Security
in
Computer Operating Systems

G O'Shea

NCC Blackwell

MANCHESTER · OXFORD

British Library Cataloguing in Publication Data

O'Shea, G
   Security in computer operating systems
   I. Title
   005.8

ISBN 0-85012-812-9

First published in 1991 by:

NCC Blackwell Limited, 108 Cowley Road, Oxford OX4 1JF, England.

Editorial Office: The National Computing Centre Limited, Oxford Road, Manchester M1 7ED, England.

Typeset in 11/13pt Palacio by M Wilson, The National Computing Centre Limited; and printed and bound in Great Britain by Biddles Limited, Guildford and King's Lynn

ISBN 1-85012-812-9

Acknowledgements

The author wishes to thank IBM and AT&T in recognition of the use of their trademarks with respect to MVS and UNIX systems as mentioned in this book.

G O'Shea
October 1991

Preface

Operating systems manage the real resources of a computer, providing useful and easy ways of using them and often allowing them to be shared between several users. In cases where access to those resources needs to be controlled, for example, to preserve the confidentiality of the data, operating systems are frequently called upon to enforce these requirements. This often results in operating systems assuming a critical role in preserving security in computer systems, particularly those that are shared between users.

Operating systems are usually large and complex pieces of software. It is difficult to provide and maintain security in such systems and the success of hackers provides simple evidence as to the vulnerabilities of many of today's operating systems to persistent, albeit simple, attacks. This can present considerable problems to anybody needing to use sophisticated or large systems in a secure manner, for commercial, military, or any other purposes. This problem has received considerable attention, largely in the form of research sponsored by military bodies, whose requirements were perceived to be more acute. The results of much of this research tended to identify and highlight the weaknesses of most general-purpose operating systems, such as those commonplace today. In order to encourage the development of commercially available systems providing adequate levels of security, evaluation schemes have been produced which aim to provide an objective assessment of a system, the best known being by the Trusted Computer System Evaluation Criteria (TCSEC) operated by the National Computer Security Center in the United States. This is a most influential force in the Information Technology market-place of today, and its influence is continuing to grow.

The foundations upon which these evaluation criteria are based are not familiar to the majority of practitioners today. Although references and claims concerning the evaluation status of their products are being made by most manufacturers, the practitioner is poorly placed to understand the implications and benefits associated with various evaluation levels without an understanding of the rationale behind them.

This book aims to provide today's practitioner with the necessary background to enable him to understand and assess the implications and usefulness of operating system security features, such as those identified in current evaluation criteria. It aims to do this in a manner that should not seem unfamiliar or daunting to anyone who has not specialised in this field. It is primarily intended for anybody concerned about the security of a computer system which they manage, or which they use.

Contents

Introduction

There are many aspects to computer security, of which this book is concerned with only one, namely the security of contemporary general-purpose operating systems. This topic is often crucial to the overall security of a computer system, but because it is specialised, tends to be an area where a large number of practitioners are unfamiliar with many of the important concepts and results available.

This book is intended for people responsibile for the preservation of security in contemporary operating systems, in particular for systems administrators, security officers, auditors and systems programmers in commercial installations.

The intention of this book is to cover important issues in operating systems security, many of which are buried away in research papers and specialist journals that few people have ready access to. By presenting these in a form that is easily understood, it hopes to dispel much of the mysticism and uncertainty that surrounds the subject.

Most of the issues covered are general, and I have tried to avoid discussing specific systems, except as examples. The concepts and mechanisms upon which individual systems are built are of a few fundamental types and it is these that this book concentrates on.

This book was produced as a companion to the earlier NCC publications *"Audit and Control of Systems Software"* and *"Computer Access Control"*, and tries not to replicate the information contained in them (*Douglas, 1983, Wood, 1985*).

Operating systems are relatively large and complex computer programs, and security (which we have yet to define) proves to be a subtle and elusive property. A wide variety of techniques have been applied in solving the problems it poses and this is reflected in the wide range of issues covered in this book. The intention is always to introduce the techniques and concepts in a form that will be illuminating and useful to the practitioner, avoiding detailed tutorials and theoretical discussions (specialist publications may be consulted for these and ample references are provided).

1 Basic concepts

1.1 INTRODUCTION

This chapter provides a basic introduction to the rest of the book by establishing a context for discussions of 'operating systems' and 'security', each of which is considered below in general terms.

1.2 WHAT IS AN OPERATING SYSTEM?

In order to give some idea of what an operating system is, first consider what a contemporary general-purpose micro-computer without an operating system would be like. For example, most people are familiar with an IBM PC compatible microcomputer. In fact, it wouldn't make much difference if we chose another type of computer, because what we are about to describe has close similarities with most contemporary computers.

Let's imagine we approach a computer, which is switched on and running, with a view to finding out what is on a floppy disk we haven't used for some time. We know that in order to find out what is on a floppy disk, on most standard PCs we have to insert the floppy disk into a drive drive and then type:

DIR A:

The screen of the PC is blank at this stage, so we insert the diskette, type in our command and press 'enter'. We immediately notice that several things that we were expecting to happen haven't happened; nothing has appeared on the screen. There is no display of what is on the diskette and even the command we typed has not appeared. There is no invitation to type on the screen, which is still completely blank. Having fiddled with the brightness and contrast controls on the screen and convinced ourselves that its cables are correctly attached, we try our command again. This time we notice something else isn't happening — the disk drive remains inactive, making no attempt to read our diskette.

1

In short, the computer will not listen to us, it won't speak to us and it clearly isn't doing anything useful with the expensive if somewhat temperamental 'features' that convinced us it was a particularly good bargain when we bought it.

Suppose that we know that the diskette has got some programs on it, which we know we can run on the PC down the corridor. Why can't we run these in our seemingly unfriendly computer?

The first hurdle is that we need to read the programs from the diskette and at the moment the computer won't read anything (in fact there isn't any way for us to tell it to try).

Suppose we could overcome this somehow, and copy a program from our diskette into the computer and start it running. What would happen then? The answer is, probably not a lot. In most cases, the program will not have been written to handle the machinery (hardware) of our computer directly — it would expect some other program within the computer to do that for it. Just like the person at the keyboard, the program would be expecting the computer to provide a convenient medium for conversation to take place, and the computer will play dead just as it did with the command at the keyboard.

All of this should start to give some idea of what an operating system does for us and for the programs we run in a computer. Much of the time, what we see as 'the computer', in terms of messages displayed on a screen, is put there by the operating system. Similarly, many of the things that we (and the programs we run) expect to find in the computer, such as files and commands, only exist because of the operating system installed in the computer.

All in all, a computer without an operating system is about as intelligent as a fridge (philosophers may wish to dispute this).

1.3 A RATHER SPECIAL PROGRAM

Once we understand where the operating system fits into the grand design of our computer, we can start to think about what it is.

So what is it?

The simple answer is 'a program'. In the final analysis that's all it is, but we realise that it is somewhat different from the majority of programs which are written and we would like to recognise this. So, remembering what a computer without an operating system doesn't do, we can begin by offering a couple of guidelines.

An operating system:

- manages the real hardware mechanisms of a computer;

- provides convenient and useful views of a computer to its users, whether they be people or programs.

We can think of another layer on top of the operating system, and that is the programs we choose to run in the computer (the program that displays things on the screen and interprets our commands is not usually part of the operating system proper — more often it is a program written purely for that purpose).

1.4 SOME HISTORY

Early computers provided very little in the way of an operating system, so programmers had to worry about all the details of the computer hardware in their programs. This was not very convenient for the programmer and did not allow for efficient use of the computer, as each program would occupy it completely and a good deal of the capacity of the computer was idle for much of the time. This was unsatisfactory because early computers were very expensive and in considerable demand.

Early attempts to address some of these issues provided library routines for handling hardware, and spooling systems for buffering input and output from the computer. More sophisticated developments introduced the concept of *multi-tasking*, where several programs can coexist within the computer, taking turns to use the processor (assuming there is only one processor). This allowed much more efficient use of the processor, which no longer had to remain idle waiting for the relatively slow input and output devices to catch up.

The advent of spooling and multi-programming, and the stabilisation of routines for handling hardware operations, were early events in the evolution of operating systems. They were significant also in that they introduced a much higher degree of sharing into the computing environment. The implications of this sharing cannot be overstated, both from a pragmatic and a security perspective.

Taking a pragmatic viewpoint, one has to be able to place programs in different parts of memory and still have them work properly. This means that the addresses they use internally must be independent of physical hardware addresses, and early memory management techniques were developed to handle this. It was also found necessary to provide some way of isolating the addresses used by one program from those of another; if only to prevent errors in one program from corrupting other programs (including the operating system). Hardware techniques were developed to provide the necessary protection mechanisms in the computer hardware, and the concept of a 'privileged' state of program execution was introduced so that only the operating system could perform the operations that were critical to maintaining the protection mechanisms.

As the power of computers increased, the degree of sharing increased. As the utility of computers increased, the value of data held in them increased. The need to protect data against corruption and disclosure increased and placed further demands on the protection mechanisms and the software that control sharing.

Current large operating systems are the result of several decades of development, which have seen their functions and size increase dramatically. This has not always been in the best interests of their security, as some of the largest and most common operating systems are so complex and difficult to maintain that it seems unlikely they will ever be very secure.

On the other hand, we can see striking similarities between the operating systems on early mainframe computers and today's personal computers. Many modern PCs run the PC-DOS or MS-DOS operating systems (much the same thing, in fact). These were developed to run on a microprocessor that did not provide any protection features. At the time it did not matter because the microprocessors and memory available to it were limited, so it was acceptable not to allow any sharing. Thus programs were run one at a time in a dedicated machine, and that is all that MS-DOS was designed and written to support.

Years later, the same family of microprocessors does provide protection mechanisms, and the power of the hardware can easily support multi-tasking in many cases. MS-DOS however, can still only run the computer in dedicated mode and because it does not use the protection mechanisms they might as well not be there.

As a result of MS-DOS not controlling the co-existence of programs in its memory, and because it does not use the protection mechanisms to protect files on disk, PCs are vulnerable to programs that deliberately try to interfere with other programs or files, for example, computer viruses.

The need for protection mechanisms within computers has been recognised and understood for decades, and yet many of todays computers ignore this in the design of their operating system. The emergence of a family of programs that cause corruption by exploiting this vulnerability (virus programs) seems entirely predictable, human nature being what it is. Since we know there is a fundamental requirement for protection in computers that has been ignored, we must accept the consequences of our decision to use these computers, ie that there is a risk of viruses which we cannot control. The danger is somewhat analogous to driving a car that we know has no brakes fitted.

1.5 FEATURES OF OPERATING SYSTEMS

Computers come in many shapes and sizes, and so do the operating systems that control them. Among the more significant factors distinguishing one type of operating system from another are:

- support for multi-programming (or multi-tasking);

- support for more than one user;

- the number and power of the features offered by the operating system;

- support for inter-working of operating system services and applications-over-networks;

- support for distributed processing;

- support for multi-processor configurations;

- the design of the operating system.

Equally, there are a number of features that most operating systems of interest have in common:

- management of primitive hardware, including controlled sharing of Input/Output devices, memory and processors;

- provision of 'abstract' resources such as files, memory segments and processes;

- provision of services and utilities, such as spoolers, command interpreters and editors.

Many operating systems are specialised. This book attempts to cover the most useful cases by assuming that an operating system is 'multi-user' and 'general-purpose'; meaning that several different people can use it for a wide variety of purposes. Most data processing, program development and office systems come into this category. The issues covered will often equally apply to specialised operating systems, and the reader should have little trouble in identifying when this is the case.

The relative importance of the issues covered in this book depends largely upon the design of a particular system and the circumstances in which it is used. For example, issues of network security (such as 'peer-entity authentication' and detection of 'message stream modification') are of increased importance in networked and distributed systems. Again, once the issues have been understood, the reader should be able to identify the salient points in a particular situation.

The need for security features in an operating system may be identified as a result of security policy requirements and risk analysis exercises. Threats to various assets within the system may thus be reduced to an acceptable level, often cost-justified in terms of the value of the asset being protected and the cost of the counter-measure being adopted. However, security policies and risk analysis techniques are beyond the intended scope of this book.

1.6 THE CONCEPT OF SECURITY

A variety of loose definitions of security exist in the literature. For example, that security concerns the ability to protect information of value and to uphold rights of individual privacy.[1] Alternatively, security may be defined as a measure of confidence concerning the preservation of integrity, both of data and of the system itself.[2] Or, that security is concerned with ensuring the uncorrupted and uninterrupted functioning of systems that provide a useful service.[3] Clearly, various notions of security exist. A reasonably informal definition is given in the *Trusted Computer System Evaluation Criteria*:

> "Any discussion of computer security necessarily starts from a statement of requirements, ie what it really means to call a computer system 'secure'. In general, secure systems will control, through use of specific security features, access to information that only properly authorized individuals, or processes operating on their behalf, will have access to read, write, create, or delete information." (Department of Defense Computer Security Center, 1983).

Some other useful definitions of security are given in the Open Systems Interconnection documentation, and in the various draft documents issued by the Department of Trade and Industry Commercial Computer Security Centre.

Open Systems Interconnection (OSI)

OSI uses the term security to imply that weaknesses which could be exploited to violate a system or the information it protects have been addressed.[4] The draft Department of Trade and Industry security evaluation criteria issued in 1989 defined security as:

- "confidentiality, the prevention of the unauthorised disclosure of information;

- integrity, the prevention of the unauthorised amendment or deletion of information;

- availability, the prevention of the unauthorised withholding of information or resources."[5]

These issues of confidentiality, integrity and availability often occur in discussions of computer security. Common meanings of these terms are summarised below.

Confidentiality

Confidentiality of information is concerned with ensuring that information is only disclosed to authorised parties. This is an obvious requirement of any security policy concerned with 'privacy' or 'secrecy' of data or of information, and is related to the generic READ access present in many file systems.

Confidentiality requirements have been paramount in much of the research sponsored by military concerns and are consequently the best served of the security requirements in operating systems.

Integrity

Integrity of information is often cited as the most important aspect of security in commercial systems. As a simple example, it might be related to the generic WRITE access in file systems that may be used to prevent data modification by unauthorised processes. It is also concerned with the system's ability to ensure information correctness across system component failures; thus in sophisticated examples concerns the trust placed in processes 'or other entities' to provide correct information (ie with the quality of the information — which is not addressed in classical information theory). Implicitly, integrity is concerned with protecting the system from adverse (unauthorised or unintended) effects of user processes, and equally with protecting processes from each other.

Availability

Availability is concerned with ensuring that information is available whenever it is required. This is related to the systems ability to confine and recover from faults, and its ability to continue in degraded mode (that is, the system is 'survivable'). In a similar fashion to integrity, this continuity implies protecting the operating system and processes from the adverse effects of unauthorised actions, so that continuity of service is not unduly impaired as a result.

Generally, security in operating systems concerns the ability of the operating system to enforce control over the storage and movement of information in and between the objects that the operating system supports and manages.[6] A security policy will reflect the requirements of the organisation using the computer system, and indeed may be directly derived from the rules and regulations governing that organisation.[7] The ability to call a system secure depends upon a precise security policy,[8] and if a system can model and enforce this policy, then it may justifiably be called secure.

It is clear that 'security' is a pervasive property which cannot be treated in isolation, particularly where high degrees of security are required. The ability of contemporary systems to provide high degrees of integrity or continuity is limited, although security requirements impose a rigour on operating system design and implementation that is not otherwise often observed. The development of secure systems has required exploitation of software engineering practices to the limit of current knowledge and technology; particularly in the areas of design, verification and implementation.

Already we can make an important observation with respect to operating system security. Multi-user operating systems are required to implement sharing of resources, while security is largely concerned with separation. Sharing and separation are essentially opposites, so that considerable tension is introduced into the design of any system required to support both. To achieve these seemingly conflicting requirements, the operating system must ensure that the only way users (or rather, the programs acting on their behalf) can interact with shared resources or with each other is subject to controls enforced by the operating system.

The first step is to arrange it so that shared resources are protected from direct access by users, and that user programs cannot interfere with each other or with the operating system. This is achieved through the use of various types of protection mechanism, which are described in Chapter 4. User programs now have to access shared resources via the operating system (possibly indirectly, via some form of trusted software). This is usually achieved by some form of system call mechanism for directly invoking operating system functions. The operating system is now able to limit the access it will allow to meet security objectives that have been expressed to it.

This boundary between the operating system and user programs is most important. Protection mechanisms must be used to ensure that this boundary affords real protection to the operating system within it, so that user programs cannot damage or circumvent its controls. (The lack of protection mechanisms in most contemporary personal computers leaves their operating system and critical resources open to corruption by user programs, and virus programs prey on this vulnerability.) The operating system itself usually carries some responsibility in this area, since it must ensure that the system calls and other services it offers to user programs do not contain weaknesses that could be used to circumvent the desired controls. The boundary is usually referred to as the '*TCB boundary*', for reasons that will become clear later.

Operating system security is critically dependent on all that lies within it and all the mechanisms that protect the boundary or offer services that transcend it. For many practical purposes we can regard the TCB boundary as defining the operating system itself.

Notes:

1   JAN 87a
2   Pet 83a, p387
3   Dei 84a, p447
4   ISO 88a/ISO 89a
5   DTI 896, DTI 89C
6   Jon 79b
7   DoD 83a
8   Dei 84a, p448

(*see* Reference section).

2   Security evaluation and security policies

2.1 INTRODUCTION

This chapter provides an introduction to the most important of the public computer security evaluation criteria.

Security evaluation criteria are proving to be a significant influence on commercial computer systems. The influence arises primarily due to the marketing advantage of being able to claim conformance with recognised evaluation criteria and because large organisations (particularly government and military bodies) are starting to insist upon conformance before they will accept a system.

A number of schemes supporting evaluation and certification of computer systems against security criteria have been proposed and introduced. The most influential of these are discussed below.

2.2 THE TRUSTED COMPUTER SYSTEM EVALUATION CRITERIA

A significant initiative was taken in 1983 in the United States of America by the National Computer Security Center (the NCSC, formerly known as the Department of Defense Computer Security Center)[1] The NCSC formulated a set of security criteria for use by United States government and military organisations called the *'Trusted Computer System Evaluation Criteria'*, also commonly referred to as the 'TCSEC' or the *'Orange Book'*.

A fundamental objective was to encourage the development of secure systems by commercial suppliers, and so a centre was established for evaluating systems against the criteria and publishing the results. The TCSEC has been a major influence on security in commercially available systems, with most major suppliers keen to enhance their products to meet various levels within the criteria. However, the principles behind the criteria are not universally accepted as appropriate outside of the US government and military environments, largely because they do not directly address integrity issues.

Background

The background to the formulation of the TCSEC was the need to provide systems for US government and military institutions, many of which have stringent security requirements. The re-quirements for such systems were reasonably well defined, and military sponsorship of security-related research projects meant that systems meeting these requirements were reasonably well understood. Table 2.1 indicates important developments that preceded the formulation of the TCSEC, some of which are reviewed in a later chapter.

The result of these research projects was a reasonable understanding of what was achievable and practical in the area of operating systems meeting the specific security requirements concerned. This left the problem that such systems were not readily available for use.

The TCSEC and its associated certification scheme was thus intended as an incentive aimed at encouraging the developers and suppliers of computing systems to produce systems that would meet these requirements. The ready availability of such systems would allow the widespread adoption of systems with improved security properties within the US military and government environments, at a reasonable cost.

The TCSEC

The TCSEC was developed to:

- Provide a metric for evaluation of security properties in computer systems;

- Provide guidelines for system developers;

- Establish standards that may be used in procurement specifications.

Systems are submitted to the National Computer Security Center for evaluation against the TCSEC, and an evaluated products list is published by the Center.

YEAR	DEVELOPMENTS
1964-67	MULTICS Development (MIT)
1972-74	Bell and LaPadula Models (MIT)
1972-75	MULTICS Access Isolation Mechanism (AIM) Development
1975	SCOMP (Honeywell)
1975-77	MULTICS Kernel project UCLA Secure Unix PSOS (SRI) (not implemented — no suitable hardware) KSOS-II (Ford Aerospace PDP-11)
1976	KVM/370 (System Development Corp)
1981	DoD Computer Security Center founded
1983	TCSEC

Table 2.1 Chronology of developments prior to TCSEC

Six fundamental requirements are identified in the criteria as essential in achieving computer system security.

1. An explicit and precise security policy must be defined and enforced by the system.

2. Every object subject to the security policy must be marked with an access control label.

3. Individual subjects accessing information must be identified.

4. A protected audit trail of security-related actions must be maintained.

5. The hardware and software mechanisms enforcing the above requirements must be open to independent evaluation determining the degree of confidence that can be placed in them.

6. The hardware and software mechanisms must be continuously protected against unauthorised alteration.

The TCSEC describes the need for a 'Security Policy Control Objective', which is defined as 'A statement of intent with regard to control over access to and dissemination of information, to be known as the security policy'.[2]

It places emphasis on preserving the confidentiality (or secrecy) of information. This emphasis has influenced the design of most secure operating systems, since most research and development effort has been directed towards achieving this objective.

The original TCSEC document describes a set of security controls that can be applied more or less directly to a general purpose operating system running on a single computer. Having adapted the TCSEC, it has been necessary to produce various interpretations and guidelines for those cases that are not single computer operating systems, such as networked operating systems and databases. Amongst the supporting documentation in what has become known as the 'rainbow series' or 'the salad bowl' (thanks to the range of colours used for the covers) are a Trusted Network Interpretation, a Trusted Database Interpretation, password guidelines, guidelines on discretionary access controls and the Evaluated Products List of systems that have completed or are undergoing evaluation.

Mandatory and discretionary policies

The TCSEC differentiates between mandatory (MAC) and discretionary (DAC) security policies and the controls that enforce them. Discretionary access control allow access to objects (and hence information flow) on the basis of action taken by subjects owning or accessing the object. This is the conventional form of protection mechanism, and is used in low classes of security systems and to provide refinements in addition to mandatory controls. Mandatory access control provide access control irrespective of the discretionary actions taken by individual users or processes. This makes it possible to place greater reliance on the correctness of access controls, and addresses risks such as 'Trojan Horse' software which might attempt to breach the security policy.

The mandatory policy expected by the TCSEC is a Multi-level Security or MLS policy, which will be discussed in greater detail later. The MLS policy is an expression of the regulations and controls used in the US military environment. It has been formally expressed in mathematical models such as the *Bell and LaPadula Model* and various derivations thereof. The Bell and LaPadula Model is concerned with access control between subjects and objects[3] and recognises read, write, execute and read-write access relationships between these two types of objects.

Reference Monitor

The TCSEC expects that a system will implement the concept of a 'reference monitor', in order to enforce security policy, defining a reference monitor as being responsible for enforcing authorised access relationships between subjects and objects within the system.

A 'reference validation mechanism' is described as an implementation of the reference monitor concept. Three design requirements are stated for such mechanisms:

'(a) The reference validation mechanism must be tamper proof.

(b) The reference validation mechanism must always be invoked.

(c) The reference validation mechanism must be small enough to be subject to analysis and testing, the completeness of which can be assured.'[4]

A system designed and implemented strictly according to these criteria is said to implement a security kernel, and such systems tend to have achieved the highest assurance of security. Most systems implement a 'reference validation mechanism' as part of a general purpose mechanism (ie an operating system) whose size and complexity precludes conformance with item (c) above. To cater for such systems, which are in the majority, the TCSEC also describes the concept of a Trusted Computing Base (TCB), which it defines as that part of the system which contains all the elements of the system that are responsible for supporting and enforcing security policy. This definition allows mechanisms other than those concerned with security to reside within the TCB, but does not permit security critical mechanisms to reside outside of the TCB. Although a TCB may thus be an extremely large and complex mechanism, the TCSEC encourages simplicity in TCBs in order that greater assurances as to its completeness and correctness can be obtained.

The four divisions of TCSEC

The TCB concept proves to be extremely useful when reviewing the structure and mechanism of an operating system.

TCSEC is structured into four divisions against which systems are evaluated, where the requirements of a given division includes all the requirements of all lower divisions.

The divisions are:

> D – Minimal Protection, ie less than division C
>
> C – Discretionary Protection
>
> B – Mandatory Protection
>
> A – Verified Protection

Increasing demands in terms of the fundamental security requirements lead to divisions C and B being further divided into two and three classes respectively. In all cases, the stringency of testing conducted during evaluation increases in keeping with the stringency of the division and class involved.

The TCSEC introduces a number of technical concepts and mechanisms which may be unfamiliar to the reader at this stage. The reader is advised to consider reviewing this section again after completing the remainder of the book.

Division D

This division is reserved for systems that have failed to meet the evaluation criteria of any higher division.

Class C1 – Discretionary Security Protection

Class C1 nominally satisfies the requirements of a discretionary Security System by separating users and data. Class C1 is described as representing 'good commercial practice', and is intentionally aimed at those types of system supporting cooperating users of the same or similar security classifications.

The major criteria requirements are as follows:

- *Security Policy:* The TCB controls access between named users and objects, such that users may control access to objects on the basis of named individuals or group users.

- *Accountability:* The TCB enforces user identification, with authentication by a protected mechanism — such as a password mechanism. Authentication data must be protected from unauthorised access.

- *Assurance:* The system architecture must maintain a domain for TCB execution such that it is protected from unauthorised modification of its code or data. The TCB may only be required to protect a subset of the system objects. Facilities must be provided to allow periodic validation of the TCB operations. Conformance testing is by two Computer Science graduates over one to three months, and must ensure that no obvious ways to penetrate the TCB protection mechanisms are apparent.

- *Documentation:* This must be provided on use of the TCB features, privileged facilities requiring controlled use, the developers testing results and the philosophy and implementation of the TCB protection mechanisms. If applicable, the modularity of the TCB must be described.

Class C2 – Controlled Access Protection

Class C2 is concerned with finer granularity of discretionary access controls, with a fundamental requirement for individual accountability of users enforced by login procedures, protected audit trails of security related events and isolation of security related objects by the TCB.

The additional requirements of class C2 above those of C1 are given below.

- *Security Policy:* Access controls are applied to individuals, or group of identifiable individuals, and must be capable of granting or refusing object access at the request of an individual user. The TCB must ensure that re-usable objects do not contain residual data when allocated, for example, that disk blocks do not contain data from a previously deleted file.

— *Accountability:* The TCB is able to enforce individual accountability through unique identification and protected audit trails. The TCB must maintain audit information on use of identification/authentication mechanisms (to include origin of request eg terminal ID), object access, object deletion and the activities of operators, system administrators and security officers.

   The audit trail information must include the relevant date and time, user identity, type of event, success or failure of event, and object name. The system administrator must be able to selectively audit activities on the basis of individual user names.

— *Assurance:* The TCB must isolate protected resources to ensure access controls and audit requirements are enforced.

— *Documentation:* Procedures must be documented for examining and maintaining the audit trails, and the record structure of audit data must be described.

Class B1 — Labelled Security Protection

Class B1 requires an informal security model to be defined and that data should be labelled and subject to mandatory access controls. Class B1 is believed to be achievable on most modern systems, by retrofit of features to a C2 certified system.

   IBM's VM and MVS operating systems (with the RACF product installed) have been targeted for B1 classification[5] and ICL claims that its VME operating system with the High Security Option installed is equivalent to a B1 certified system. Both cases appear to confirm the above beliefs concerning B1 potential.

— *Security Policy:* All objects under the control of the TCB must have sensitivity labels, and be subject to mandatory access controls. Authorised users are required to establish sensitivity labels for data, and these are unambiguously attached to exported information.

Every Input/Output (I/O) channel or device is labelled as single-level or multi-level by an authorised user, and data exported to a multi-level device must unambiguously include its security label. The exportation of security labels is applied to printed output, such that each page is marked with the highest sensitivity of information appearing in it. The various sensitivity labels are used to enforce and reflect the Multi-Level Security (MLS) mandatory access control policy.

— *Accountability:* The TCB maintains the information relating security labels to users and also to the objects they create. Audit mechanisms are extended to record security labels in audit data and to record override of printed output markings.

— *Assurance:* The TCB is required to enforce process isolation through distinct address spaces under its control. Conformance testing by two computer science graduates and a holder of a Masters degree must ensure that no flaws exist whereby unauthorised read, write or delete access can be obtained to any object under the control of the TCB. It must not be possible for any unauthorised subject to cause the TCB to fail to respond to communications initiated by any other subject. An informal or formal model of the TCB security policy must be provided, which must be shown to be consistent with its axioms.

— *Documentation:* Documentation must cover the security related functions of system administrators and operators. Further, it must describe how to effectively use the protection mechanisms of the system, the facilities and privileges needing control, and the procedure for securely regenerating a TCB. The protection mechanisms in use must be related to the security model, with some explanation of how these enforce the security model.

Class B2 – Structured Protection

Class B2 requires the TCB to be based on a formal security policy model, and to control all objects within the system. The TCB design must separate protection-critical components from other components of the TCB, and must be amenable to thorough testing and review. It is considered unlikely, although not impossible, that a highly engineered existing system could achieve B2 certification.

Normally a B2 system (and certainly those at higher classifications) is expected to have been designed and implemented specifically with the required security properties as specific goals. Authentication mechanisms are strengthened, covert information channels are addressed, and stringent configuration management controls are enforced. The following requirements exist above those of class B1.

- *Security Policy:* All objects are labelled and subject to mandatory and discretionary access controls. Terminal users are informed of changes in security level, and may enquire the current level of the TCB. All physical devices attached to the system are labelled to reflect physical environmental considerations.

- *Accountability:* The TCB supports a trusted path between itself and terminal users for purposes of identification and authentication, with these operations initiated solely by the user. Events that may signify use of covert channels are audited.

- *Assurance:* The TCB is structured so that architectural features such as address space separation and storage controls (such as segmentation) are used to isolate protection-critical components from all others and to enforce a principle of least privilege. The developer must have conducted a search for covert channels and estimated the bandwidth of those found.

  The system must support separate operator and administrator functions. A formal model of the TCB security policy must be available, and a Descriptive Top-Level Specification (DTLS) must be provided that describes the TCB in terms of its effects and exception messages. Evaluation testing must demonstrate that the model and DTLS accurately describe the TCB, that the TCB is relatively resistant to penetration and that all discovered flaws have been removed without introducing any new flaws. A configuration management system must describe how effectively covert channels have been controlled, and must state the bandwidths of any remaining covert channels.

- *Documentation:* The TCB components that constitute the reference monitor must be identified, and the procedures for generating a new TCB described. Test documentation must describe the effectiveness with which covert channels have been reduced and their remaining bandwidths. The design documentation must describe the correctness and effectiveness of the TCB in implementing the reference monitor concept, the structure of the TCB, the events used in covert channel analysis.

Class B3 – Security Domains

The TCB in class B3 systems must be engineered for minimal complexity. A security administrator role must be supported, secure recovery procedures must be provided and the system must be highly resistant to penetration attempts.

- *Security Policy:* Discretionary access to objects must be controlled at the granularity of individual users (or groups thereof), but now including the mode of access, and also providing for specific exclusion of access by an individual (or group).

- *Accountability:* A trusted path between TCB and user must be provided for operations such as log-in and requests to change the current security level (to prevent the user being deceived by untrustworthy code that emulates a log-on password check, for example). The TCB must monitor events that may indicate impending security violation, and notify a security administrator when thresholds are breached.

- *Assurance:* The TCB must be structured to use simple and precise protection mechanisms, and must employ significant layering, abstraction and data-hiding in its design. The TCB must support the role of security administrator, which can only be assumed following distinct and auditable action. Breaks in system service must be recovered by procedures that ensure the preservation of security. During testing, no design flaws are permitted and only a minimal number of minor implementation flaws are allowed.

- *Documentation:* The documentation must include procedures for the secure start-up and recovery of the system. Informal techniques must be used to show that the TCB is consistent with the DTLS and that the elements of both correspond.

Class A1 – Verified Design

Class A1 does not introduce any new functions beyond those of class B3, but requires the use of formal methods in the specification, design, modelling and analysis of the system. In this respect class A1 differs from the classes below it, each of which introduces additional functional requirements. Class A1 otherwise continues the general theme of increasing assurances of security at higher levels within the TCSEC.

- *Security policy:* identical requirements to those of class B3.

- *Accountability:* identical requirements to those of Class B3.

- *Assurance:* Formal methods must be used to search for covert channels. A Formal Top Level Specification (FTLS) must be supplied, and mapped (possibly manually) down to source code level. The FTLS must describe the TCB effects, error messages and exceptions, including those parts of the TCB implemented in hardware or microcode. The FTLS must be shown to be consistent with the security model, and together with the construction tools used, must be subject to a strict configuration management throughout its entire development.

  Master copies of the system must be closely guarded, and secure distribution procedures adopted to ensure that master copies and on-site copies of the current TCB version remain consistent.

- *Documentation:* Test documentation must show the mapping between the FTLS and source code. Elements of hardware, microcode and software internal to the TCB but not dealt with in the FTLS must be clearly described. Evaluation testing must be conducted over a three to six month period.

Beyond Class A1

The criteria allow for systems beyond class A1, suggesting such considerations as self-protection and completeness for reference monitors, as yet unattainable formal specification, verification and implementation techniques, and design by trusted personnel.

2.3 THE OSI SECURITY ADDENDUM

The growing interest in open systems and the continuing development of products which meet standards for Open Systems Inter-connection (OSI) has important implications for security requirements in operating systems. Interconnected systems share much of the responsibility for security between different connected systems, and often shift much of the emphasis towards addressing the vulnerability of the connecting communication links.

OSI standards documents discuss issues of security in an addendum to the basic OSI architectural reference model. The security requirements and appropriate techniques for providing these are essentially concerned with communications issues, as they occur at different levels of the OSI model, while our concerns in respect of operating system security are largely those of an OSI application. However, since an increasing number of systems will use networked operating systems, those operating systems will need to employ suitable mechanisms to address the security risks introduced.

In many cases OSI compliant operating systems will be able to exploit OSI security services, and for this reason it seems appropriate to at least introduce the OSI security concepts at this point. Most of the OSI mechanisms are exemplified in the techniques described later in this book. The terminology differs somewhat, but the concepts and techniques are easily recognised.

The main theme of the OSI security addendum relates to networking issues, and the reader may consult specialist publications on network security for a more detailed discussion of security than space permits here. The OSI security addendum describes fourteen security services, and identifies those levels of the OSI reference model at which they are considered appropriate. It also identifies eight mechanisms that may be employed to provide the various security services. We will restrict ourselves to a brief introduction to each of the services and mechanisms.

OSI Security Services

The security services described for OSI are:

- Peer entity authentication, which assures the identity of some remote party.

- Data origin authentication, which assures that data (eg a message) has indeed come from the claimed source.

- Access control services, providing access control to all manner of network objects, including sessions being requested to (or from) a remote entity.

- Connection confidentiality, ensuring the confidentiality of all data in a communication session between two entities.

- Connectionless confidentiality, ensuring the secrecy of data sent between parties that have not established a communication session (for example, because the protocols they are using do not support connection-oriented sessions).

- Selective field confidentiality, ensuring the confidentiality of data in selected fields within a communication transfer.

- Traffic flow confidentiality, preventing the disclosure of information by analysis of network loading and message routing.

- Connection integrity with recovery, assuring that data is correctly transferred in the appropriate sequence and without modification, with recovery attempted in the event of problems being detected.

- Connection integrity without recovery, similar to the above but with no attempt to recover from problems (these are merely reported to the user).

- Connectionless integrity, assuring the correct transfer of data in the absence of a connection, although a greater vulnerability to replay old messages exists than is the case with connection oriented protocols.

- Selective field connectionless recovery, similar to the above but applying to only selected fields within a message.

- Non-repudiation of origin, assuring that the sender of a message cannot subsequently deny having sent it, typically by incorporating data that only the sender could have produced.

- Non-repudiation of delivery, assuring that the receiver of a message cannot subsequently deny having received it, typically by using a similar technique to the above but applied to the acknowledgement of message receipt.

OSI Security Mechanisms

The eight security mechanisms identified in the OSI security addendum are:

- Encipherment, with both DES and RSA being among the recognised algorithms.

- Digital signature, using public-key encipherment or some form of trusted intermediary.

- Access control mechanisms.

- Data integrity, using error detection mechanisms. sequence numbering, time-stamping and similar techniques in communication protocols.

- Authentication exchange, using message exchanges incorporating values that assure the identity of the parties concerned.

- Traffic padding, which includes redundancy in messages or message streams to prevent traffic analysis.

- Routing control, to direct communication traffic around insecure parts of a network.

- Notarisation, involving the use of a trusted third party capable of testifying the correctness of critical aspects of communication between different entities.

2.4 THE TRUSTED NETWORK INTERPRETATION OF THE TCSEC

The Trusted Network Interpretation of the TCSEC, otherwise known as the TNI, provides an interpretation of the TCSEC that applies to networked systems.[6] It identifies additional considerations including issues of network security, denial of service, transmission security and encryption protocols. The TCSEC considers the properties of a single, well-formed system. The network interpretation identifies that two alternate views may apply to a networked system.

1. In a 'single trusted system' view, the system is treated as a complete entity. In such a view there is a need to identify the equivalent of a TCB. This may exist as several partitions, in which case it is referred to as a 'Network Trusted Computing Base (NTCB) partition'. Each of these partitions is responsible for enforcing security policy for that part of the

system within which it resides. It is then required to show that the sum total of the NTCB partitions enforce the overall security policy required for the complete system.

2. The 'Interconnected accredited' view of a networked system considers systems as discrete components, loosely bound by interconnections. Such a view places far less restriction on the nature of each component system, but equally provides a much lower assurance as to the security of the overall system. This view is applicable to systems which were not designed and implemented within strict security requirements, such as most commercial systems. It is also the more likely scenario for Open Systems.[7]

The TNI emphasises the single trusted system view of a networked system. This view is much closer to that expected by the TCSEC, and is formed of two parts. Part 1 attempts to apply the TCSEC in a direct fashion to a networked system, using the 'single system view'. The complicating factors are considered in Part 2 and result in evaluation levels that are much more qualitative than those of Part 1.

The property of *integrity* in a system receives much more attention in the TNI. The TCSEC considers integrity primarily in terms of the need to protect mandatory security labels against unauthorised alteration, and what it refers to as 'overall system integrity'. The TNI introduces additional integrity requirements ensuring that information correctly flows between components of the network. These issues include correctness of message transmission, authentication of the source and destination of a message and correctness of the various data fields used to transfer user and protocol data. Another new consideration in the TNI is the introduction of the 'connection oriented abstraction'. This considers the way in which connections between components of a networked system are created, supported and managed. OSI notably supports connection-oriented security mechanisms, for example using access control mechanisms in the sending, intermediary and destination nodes to control session establishment.[8]

Network Trusted Computing Base

The concept of a TCB is retained in the TNI in the form of a Network Trusted Computing Base. The complete NTCB is required to enforce all aspects of the required security policy, but may be divided across several components within the system, which gives rise to the concept of an 'NTCB partition'.

It is sufficient that in combination the NTCB partitions support the overall network security policy, although individually their security policies may be different. When a component with an evaluated TCB is included in a networked system, the evaluated TCB boundary does not necessarily coincide with the NTCB boundary for that component. The TCB and NTCB boundaries are most likely to coincide when the relevant local and network security policies are equivalent.

The complete NTCB may be dependent upon the protocols and mechanisms used to provide reliable and secure communication between its components. This becomes an essential factor in evaluation of the system, including the consideration of how concurrent and asynchronous activity is coordinated within the system.

Individual NTCB components support one or more of four aspects of a decomposed security policy:

(a) Mandatory Access Control (MAC)

(b) Discretionary Access Control (DAC)

(c) Identification and Authentication (I)

(d) Audit (A)

The TCSEC functions required of each of these aspects do not always cover the entire range of evaluation levels. For example, DAC requirements are not substantially increased above level C2 of the TCSEC, in that two single-level components may be connected by a multi-level component that filters data passing between them. This reduces the security mechanisms required in the single-level components.

Mandatory access control

It may be insufficient for each component to provide support for the full security policy in isolation. This arises, for example, where two MAC components use a common language for mandatory security labels, but assign different meanings to the labels.

The assurances required for systems supporting a mandatory policy are currently only attainable if the NTCB partitions are disjointed. Thus all support of mandatory policy for any subject should be localised within the NTCB for that part of the system within which the subject resides. This avoids complications of global synchronisation and timing that would otherwise arise.

Discretionary Access Control

Discretionary Access Control mechanisms may be distributed across different components of the system, although this limits them to C2 criteria and below. An example is the use of 'group-of-user' protection, supporting access by a number of users from a remote site. This limits the number of users known on the server system, which could otherwise become burdensome. In such cases the DAC component of the client system is required to provide individual accountability for users accessing the networked service. Another technique involves passing user identities between DAC mechanisms. The user identity will have been authenticated by the client mechanism, and passed to the agent in a way that ensures that its confidentiality and integrity is preserved.

Identification and Authentication

Networked systems introduce a new dimension to the issue of authentication, which must now also apply to authentication of peer entities (components) within the system. In particular, the TNI identifies that authentication mechanisms must establish correct peer identities against such threats as falsification of identity and replay of the authentication protocol. Certain aspects of peer entity authentication are dependent on whether the entities concerned communicate using connection-oriented or connectionless modes. Connection oriented modes employ 'Peer Entity Authentication', which will often be supported by authentication protocols when binding occurs between the two entities. Connectionless modes involve 'Data Origin Authentication', where the source and destination of communication traffic may need to be established on a per-message basis. Suitable counter measures that may be employed in the supporting protocols include encryption schemes, time-stamping, handshaking, digital signatures and notarisation schemes.

The TNI considers how evaluated components may be combined, and how the expected functionality and evaluation level of the combined object may be derived from those of its constituent components. The properties of individually evaluated components must not be violated as a result of composition, and all essential interfaces, policies and protocol support must be preserved. The TNI rules for deriving evaluation levels recognise the evaluation level achieved by the constituent components in each functional category, but award only a single evaluation level to the composite object (notably, the DTI 'Green Book' criteria allow the individual category evaluation levels to be retained). For example, an object composed from a B2 MAC component and a C2 I component may be evaluated at B2, because the I criteria are the same at evaluation levels C2 and B2.

Integrity policy

The TNI gives a much greater recognition to integrity as a property of a computing system than the TCSEC, where issues of integrity were essentially limited to the preservation of mandatory security labels.

In this interpretation, an integrity policy addresses both intentional attempts to modify information (referred to as Message Stream Modification) and the unintentional but largely inevitable threat to transmitted information, that occurs through noise in communication systems and equipment failure. An integrity policy thus places great emphasis on the ability to write to objects, and constrains modification of information to comply with the integrity policy.

Support for the integrity policy must be provided by the NTCB, which must ensure that the mechanisms supporting the integrity policy are protected and always invoked. Assurance of these mechanisms requires that the design and implementation of the mechanisms must be shown to be adequate, and the interfaces and protocols used must be specifically tested during evaluation.

2.5 THE INFORMATION TECHNOLOGY SECURITY EVALUATION CRITERIA

The US National Computer Security Center has not been alone in devising a set of criteria for security evaluation purposes. Other notable examples have originated in Germany, France and the UK.

There are several reasons for nations producing their own evaluation schemes, amongst them:

- to avoid the awkwardness of the TCSEC when dealing with special purpose systems which may not offer all the functions expected in the TCSEC, or which offer these functions only when used in combination with other systems in, say, a distributed system;

- to decouple high assurance levels from the mechanisms described in the TCSEC. There is no reason, for example, why one should not desire a system providing only DAC controls to be developed using formal methods. The TCSEC would not cater for this — a C2 rating would be the highest achievable despite the increased assurance in the correctness of the system;

- developers and security authorities in countries other than the US may require a degree of autonomy from the US scheme, which might often discriminate in favour of US interested and priorities.

Notable among the non-US evaluation schemes is that devised and operated by the Communications Electronic Security Group (the CESG) at the Government Communications Headquarters (GCHQ) in Cheltenham, England. This scheme, described in a series of 'security Memorandum' documents, was devised to cater for the requirements of the UK government and military bodies when processing classified information.

The existence of multiple evaluation schemes is not attractive from several points of view. Suppliers are faced with costs and complications of getting their products evaluated several times by different bodies, possibly against similar sets of criteria. Procurers may be artificially restricted in their choice of solutions because a product has not been evaluated by the right body. At an international level this may take some time to resolve, except where a group of countries are committed to working closely together. A case in point is the European Community, where a common approach would help to ensure a consistent approach throughout the Community and allow mutual recognition of evaluation results to support regulatory requirements extending beyond single member states.

The EC has resolved this problem by producing and issuing the Information Technology Security Evaluation Criteria, or ITSEC (ITSEC91). The ITSEC harmonises the concepts of the various preceding national criteria such as those of the CESG, which it replaces. Member nations establish evaluation and certification schemes for applying ITSEC. The UK scheme has been effective since mid-1991, using Commercial Licensed Evaluation Facilities (CLEF) (CLEFs-approved software houses) to perform evaluations which are then ratified by a joint CESG/DTI body which issues the official certification reports.

The ITSEC has clearly been strongly influenced by the CESG evaluation criteria. Its evaluation levels and its approach towards specification of security functionality are almost indistinguishable. The ITSEC thus acquires the well-founded knowledge and experience captured in the CESG criteria. ITSEC also contains provisions for evaluating systems against a set of criteria that are equivalent to those of the TCSEC. The importance of this cannot be understated, as many computer products have been, and will continue to be, evaluated against the TCSEC.

The ITSEC provisions for accommodating TCSEC evaluation levels establishes a potential foundation for eventual mutual recognition and acceptance of TCSEC and ITSEC evaluation results.

Functionality and Assurance

ITSEC separates the concepts of functionality, describing what a system does, from confidence in the correctness of the system. This allows ITSEC to be applied to specialised computer components with low or high correctness requirements.

The functional aspects of a system are not prescribed by ITSEC. It is up to the sponsor of an ITSEC evaluation to state what the system (referred to as the 'Target of Evaluation' or TOE) does, and this statement is known as the 'security target'. ITSEC states how security targets should be formulated, and how they may relate to security policies for a specific installation or to general assumptions about the environment for a product that may be used in a variety of circumstances.

The purpose of the ITSEC evaluation process is to provide a statement of assurance concerning the ability of a product or system to meet its TOE. Seven levels of assurance are available, known as E0 (the lowest) through to E6 (the highest). At each level there are two aspects of assurance. The first is correctness, which is largely concerned with how rigorously the system has been developed and tested; the second aspect is effectiveness. The evaluation can be applied to a commercial product which many organisations may choose to deploy, or it can be applied to a specific example of a system, including its users and its specific security risks, to see whether the system is effective in meeting these specific requirements in practice (ITSEC refers to these cases as 'products' and 'systems' respectively).

The *ITSEC effectiveness aspects* consider whether the security functions are suitable, whether they work together effectively, how resistant they are to direct attack or circumvention, what vulnerabilities exist, how easy are they to use and whether the known vulnerabilities could be exploited in practice. These aspects would normally be considered towards the end of correctness evaluation.

The *ITSEC correctness aspects* are concerned with the rigour and detail applied to the development and operation of the TOE. These increase at each level, including all criteria of any lower evaluation levels. A brief characterisation of the levels follows:

Level E0: 'Inadequate' assurance only at this level.

Level E1: An informal description of the TOE architecture exists, and functional testing must have indicated that the TOE meets its security target.

Level E2: The description of the design of the TOE is extended down to a detailed level, and evidence of functional testing is evaluated. Configuration control and approved distribution procedures must be in place.

Level E3: Source code and hardware diagrams are evaluated for the security mechanisms within the TOE. In addition, evidence of the testing of the mechanisms is evaluated.

Level E4: A formal security policy model is required (these are described in later chapters). The descriptions of security functions and the TOE design must be semi-formal in style, for example, using diagrams and styles associated with methodologies such as SSADM.

Level E5: A close correspondence must be seen between the detailed design description and the source code or hardware diagrams.

Level E6: The security functions and the architectural design must be formally specified and consistent with the security policy model.

Evaluation at each of these levels involves a number of more detailed requirements, broken down to consider the development process, the development environment and the operational environment. Figures 2.1, 2.2 and 2.3 give an overview of the evaluation requirements at each level of the ITSEC.

Copies of the ITSEC can be obtained from the DTI Commercial Computer Security Centre, based at the National Physical Laboratory in Middlesex.

Requirement	Evaluation Level					
	E1	E2	E3	E4	E5	E6
Security target provided	Y	Y	Y	Y	Y	Y
Semi-formal functional specification	—	—	—	Y	Y	Y
Security policy model	—	—	—	Y	Y	Y
Formal functional specification	—	—	—	—	—	Y
Informal description of architecture	Y	Y	Y	Y	Y	Y
Semi-formal description of architecture	—	—	—	Y	Y	Y
Formal description of architecture	—	—	—	—	—	Y
Informal detailed design	—	Y	Y	Y	Y	Y
Semi-formal detailed design	—	—	—	Y	Y	Y
Optional testing evidence	Y	—	—	—	—	—
Functional testing evidence	—	Y	Y	Y	Y	Y
Source code/HW diagrams	—	—	Y	Y	Y	Y
Evidence of mechanism testing	—	—	Y	Y	Y	Y
Design/source correspondence	—	—	—	—	Y	Y

Figure 2.1 ITSEC Development Process Requirements

Requirement	Evaluation Level					
	E1	E2	E3	E4	E5	E6
Unique TOE identification	Y	Y	Y	Y	Y	Y
Configuration controls employed	—	Y	Y	Y	Y	Y
Acceptance procedures employed	—	—	Y	Y	Y	Y
Configuration control tools used	—	—	—	Y	Y	Y
Configuration control on all objects	—	—	—	—	Y	Y
Integration procedure employed	—	—	—	—	Y	Y
Integration procedure employed	—	—	—	—	Y	Y
Tools subject to configuration control	—	—	—	—	—	Y
Only well defined languages used	—	—	Y	Y	Y	Y
Compiler options documented	—	—	—	Y	Y	Y
Library source code inspected	—	—	—	—	Y	Y
Security procedures employed	—	Y	Y	Y	Y	Y

Figure 2.2 ITSEC Development Environment Requirements

Requirement	Evaluation Level					
	E1	E2	E3	E4	E5	E6
User documentation provided	Y	Y	Y	Y	Y	Y
Administration documentation	Y	Y	Y	Y	Y	Y
Configuration information	Y	Y	Y	Y	Y	Y
Delivery/sysgen procedures	Y	Y	Y	Y	Y	Y
Approved distribution procedure	—	Y	Y	Y	Y	Y
Audited sysgen procedure	—	Y	Y	Y	Y	Y
Configuration options formally defined	—	—	—	—	—	Y
Secure startup procedures	Y	Y	Y	Y	Y	Y
Disableable functions identified	—	Y	Y	Y	Y	Y
HW diagnostic procedures	—	Y	Y	Y	Y	Y
Secure restart procedures	—	—	—	Y	Y	Y

Figure 2.3 ITSEC Operational Environment Requirements

Notes:

1 DoD 83a
2 DoD 83a
3 Lan 81a
4 DoD 83a
5 IBM 88A
6 DoD 87a
7 ISO 88a/ISO 89a
8 ISO 88a/ISO 89a

(*see* Reference section).

3   Theoretical foundations

3.1 INTRODUCTION

This chapter presents some important concepts and models that apply to security in the operating system field. These provide us with insight into the nature of the problems facing us in the area of computer security. They also allow us to concisely and unambiguously describe our requirements for security, and to reason about our proposed solutions to those requirements.

For these reasons the higher evaluation classes of both the TCSEC and the ITSEC require that security policy models be produced describing the security requirement clearly, so that a definitive specification exists against which the system can be compared.

3.2 ACCESS MATRICES

An access matrix is a model of a protection system, originally intended for modelling and analysing access control mechanisms.

A computer system may be thought of as being composed of a finite set of uniquely identified objects. An object may be real, such as a register or a disk drive, or it may be abstract, such as a file or a database relation. The types of objects required depend upon which part of a system is being studied, but would typically include objects of type (process, domain), where the process has been initiated by (or on behalf of) an identified user of the system.[1]

A domain represents a protection environment, for example, the supervisor and problem states on IBM System-370 architectures are different domains as are processes operating on behalf of different users to whom different sets of files are available. A close association exists between domains and individual users of a computing system, such that the term 'subject' is often used instead of 'domain'.

A set of rights is also defined, where each object type may have one or more permissible rights associated with it, representing the possible actions that may be performed against that object. Thus, 'create', 'write', 'read' and 'delete' may be valid actions against an object of type 'file'. Other examples relate to such objects as message queues, I/O devices and magnetic media.[2] An important case is where the object is a process, in which case rights may include the sending of messages, receiving of messages and the ability to terminate the process.

An access matrix is represented by a two-dimensional matrix where each horizontal row is labelled with the name of a domain, and each vertical column is labelled with the name of an object (*see* Figures 3.1 and 3.2). Cells within the matrix record the access rights to the object in question identified along the vertical axis) available within the domain in question (identified along the horizontal axis). Thus, the objects accessible from within a domain are discerned by scanning horizontally along the row representing that domain, and the domains from which an object can be accessed are discerned by scanning down the column representing that object.

	object – a	object – b	object – c
subject – a	read	write	
subject – b	read		execute
subject – c	write		

A simple access matrix showing, for example, that subject-a has read access to object-a.

Figure 3.1 Simple Access Matrix

	supervisor code segment	processor state field	file system directory root	files owned by subject − a
subject − a (privileged state)	any	read,write	any	any
subject − b (privileged state)	any	read,write	any	none
subject − a (problem state)	any	read	read	any
subject − b (problem state)	none	read	read	any

An access matrix that differentiates between processor state protection domains.

Figure 3.2 Access Matrix Showing Processor States

	object − a	object − b
subject − a	read	read,write
subject − b	read	write

A simple access matrix showing its assumed initial state.

Figure 3.3 Access Matrix in Initial State

The final component of the conventional access matrix model is a set of operations for modifying the matrix.[3] The operations appearing in the literature differ in number and meaning, although the fundamental issues are the same. In essence, the fundamental operations concern:

- The addition of new domains, causing a new row to be added to the matrix, and also a new column if the domain is also represented as an object (*see* Figures 3.3 and 3.4).

- The deletion of a domain, causing the removal of a row, and also of a column if the domain is also represented as an object (*see* Figure 3.5).

	object – a	object – b
subject – a	read	read, write
subject – b	read	write
subject – c		

Access matrix after the introduction of a new domain, for example, by the command:

new-subject(c)

Figure 3.4 Access Matrix with New Domain

	object – a	object – b
subject – a	read	read, write
subject – c		

Access matrix after deletion of a domain, for example, by the command:

destroy-subject(b)

Figure 3.5 Access Matrix after Domain Deletion

	object – a	object – b	object – c
subject – a	read	read, write	
subject – c			

Access matrix after addition of a new object, for example, by the command:

new-object(c)

Figure 3.6 Access Matrix with New Object

- The addition of a new object causing a new column to be added (*see* Figure 3.6).

- The deletion of an object (causing a column to be removed from the matrix (*see* Figure 3.7).

- The addition of an access right into a cell (*see* Figure 3.8).

- The removal of an access right from a cell (*see* Figure 3.9).

	object – b	object – c
subject – a	read, write	
subject – c		

Access matrix after deletion of an object, for example, the command:

destroy-object(a)

Figure 3.7 Access Matrix after Object Deletion

	object – b	object – c
subject – a	read, write	read
subject – c	read	read, write

Access matrix after addition of rights into matrix cells, for example, by the commands:

grant-access (subject – a, object – c, read)
grant-access (subject – c, object – b, write)
grant-access (subject – c, object – c, read)
grant-access (subject – c, object – c, write)

Figure 3.8 Access Matrix with Rights Entered

	object – b	object – c
subject – a	write	read
subject – c		read, write

Access control matrix after removal of rights from cells, for example, by the commands:

revoke-access (subject – a, object – b, read)
revoke-access (subject – c, object – b, write)

Figure 3.9 Access Matrix with Rights Removed

These other commands may be subject to certain conditions holding, which are summarised below:

- The domain under which an object was created contains the 'owner' right for that object. This is typically the most powerful of rights in respect of an object, and allows deletion of the object, granting of rights for the object to other domains and granting of 'control' access to the current domain if the object is itself a domain. The control right itself cannot usually be transferred.

- For right R, the 'copy flag'[4] denoted R*, implies that the right may be passed to other domains, from whence it may then be copied into further domains. The right R may be copied with or without the copy flag set, but without the copy flag set cannot be further copied from other domains.

- For right R, the 'transfer-only copy flag'[5] implies that the right may be copied to another domain but is removed from the current domain in so doing.

- The 'control' right is exercised over domains, such that if domain A has control right over domain B, then A may remove access rights from B.

- 'Limited-use' rights may be considered, where n is decremented each time the right is used, and the right is removed when n reaches zero.[6]

A particular case of an access right is the right to 'enter' a domain (*see* Figure 3.10). Thus, domain B may be entered from domain A if A has the 'enter' right for B. When an enter right is exercised, the target domain becomes current and a different set of object rights comes into force (not necessarily including the right to re-enter the previous domain).

If the 'subject' concept of (domain, process) pairs is adopted, then new subjects will come into existence whenever a new process starts or an existing process enters a new domain.

	object – a	object – b	domain – a	domain – b	domain – c
domain – a	read			enter	enter
domain – b	write		return		
domain – c	write	read			

Access matrix showing rights that control state transitions between protection domains. Domains b and c may be entered from domain a, but control may then only be returned from domain b.

Figure 3.10 Access Matrix showing Protection Domain Switches

3.3 ANSA MODEL OF ACCESS CONTROL

The Advanced Network System Architecture project was an Alvey sponsored research program that studied issues relating to distributed computer systems.

ANSA models access control in terms of objects, by interposing an access control object in the binding between two objects subject to access controls.[7]

ANSA considers access control to involve three types of object:

- An access control object responsible for protection.

- An authorisation object, responsible for making the decision as to whether an access request should be allowed by an access control object.

— A security predicate object, which maintains the information required by authorisation objects in order to make access decisions.

Figure 3.11 depicts access control applied to a binding between objects OBJ A and OBJ B.

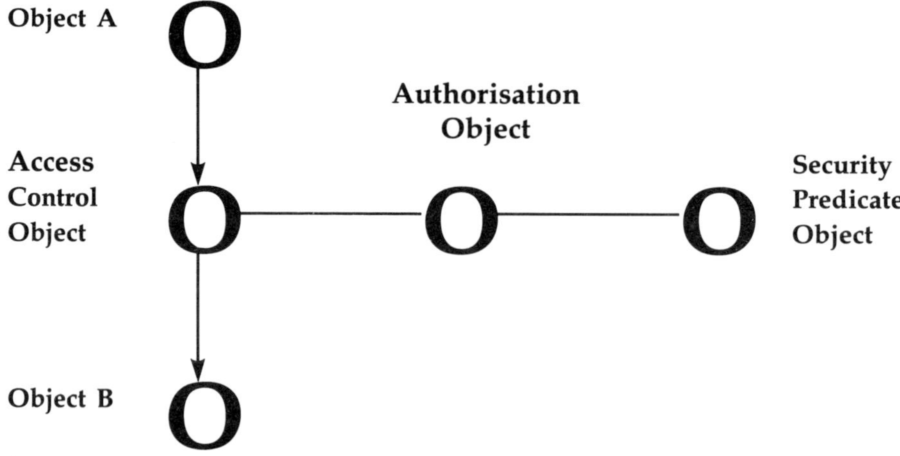

Access control is enforced between objects A and B by an Access Control Object.

Figure 3.11 ANSA Model of Access Control

In the case of an operating system, we may interpret this as having OBJA and OBJB outside of the TCB, separated using (perhaps) memory management mechanisms, with the other objects internal to the TCB. This simple model provides considerable insight into issues of protection, since it captures the essential notion of separation between objects and since the access control object may itself be decomposed into several objects modelling components of a computer system or real communication channels.

3.4 SAFE SYSTEMS

Theories relating to safe systems are concerned with abstract models of computing systems. A system is considered safe if it prevents an access right being transferred into an unauthorised protection domain. For this to be meaningful, it is usual to discount desirable (ie authorised) transfer of rights.

When we talk of a safe system in the context of computer security we are usually indicating that certain theoretical properties apply to the system in question. The theories described are important largely because they describe limitations in the use of discretionary access control mechanisms.

Mono-operational System

A mono-operational system is one in which commands that alter the state of an access matrix use only a single primitive operation. In this restricted case it can be shown that an algorithm exists for determining whether an initial configuration is unsafe for a given right. The proof relies upon showing that the number of state transitions to be considered is finite.

It is observed that all delete and destroy commands may be ignored, since commands check only for the presence of rights, and further, that the number of create commands may be reduced to one, since the rights entered into a new matrix location could be entered instead into an existing location (but allowing for an initial state containing no subjects; hence the remaining single enter command).

While the result of decidable safety in mono-operational systems shows that safety may be proven in certain cases, it is clear that few realistic systems will be mono-operational. In general, that is for an arbitrary protection system in an arbitrary state, it turns out that the question of safety is undecidable. The proof is by showing that a protection system may be defined to simulate the operation of a Turing machine, such that leakage of a given right corresponds to the Turing machine halting. The problem of determining whether an arbitrary Turing machine halts is a classic and well-known problem in computer science, and known to be undecidable, therefore, a protection system modelling such a Turing machine shows that the general safety problem is also undecidable.

The existence of a protection system of this type means that safety cannot be determined for arbitrary protection systems, hence it is necessary to consider only restricted systems when safety is deemed essential.

Take-grant Models

Take-grant models consider the transfer of rights within a protection system, and are thus also relevant to the study of the safety problem.[8] The take-grant model is based upon the use of a directed graph to model a protection system. The nodes (vertices) of the graph represent the subjects and objects of the protection system. The arcs (edges) of the graph represent, and are labelled with the access rights available between the two connected nodes, where the direction of the arc represents the application of those rights (for example, an arc from node a to node b, labelled with right r, means that a has r access to b).

Particular significance is applied to the take (t) and grant (g) rights (originally represented as r and w respectively, in a fashion comparable to reading and writing capability objects between domains).[9] State transitions in the take-grant system are modelled by rules that govern the way the graph can be changed:

The take rule allows subject a to acquire access r to object c, by taking the right from b.

Figure 3.12 The Take Rule

- The 'take' rule allows a subject to acquire access rights from another subject if the former has 'take' rights to the latter (*see* Figure 3.12).

- The 'grant' rule allows a subject to grant an access right that it possesses to some other subject, if the former has 'grant' rights to the latter (*see* Figure 3.13).

- The 'create' rule adds a new node to the graph and labels it with the rights specified on the create command.

- The 'remove' rule removes a specified right from the rights associated with a specific arc. The 'call' rule models calls between objects. If a can call b, passing parameter p, a new node n is created with 'read' access to be (ie the right to read the program file) and the appropriate access to the parameters (*see* Figure 3.14).

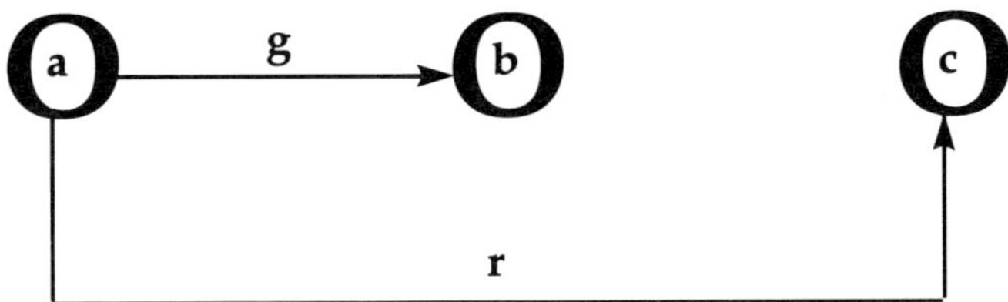

The grant rule allows subject a to grant access r to b for object c.

Figure 3.13 The Grant Rule

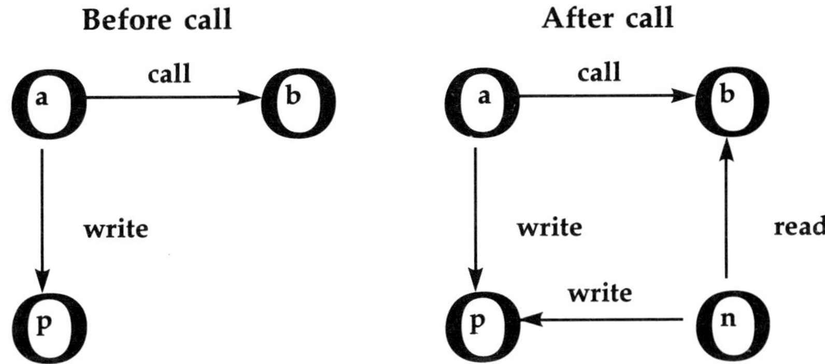

The call rule models a call from b to a, passing parameter set p. A new object n is created to represent the activation of object b.

Figure 3.14 The Call Rule

The safety-problem

The safety problem is concerned with proving whether a given right for an arbitrary object can be acquired by an arbitrary subject. If this is not the case, then the system being modelled is safe for the right and subject/objects concerned.

If nodes x and y have a path between them of arcs labelled with either take or grant rights, they are said to be tg-connected. If there is a single arc between x and y labelled with take or grant, then x and y are said to be directly tg-connected.

a)

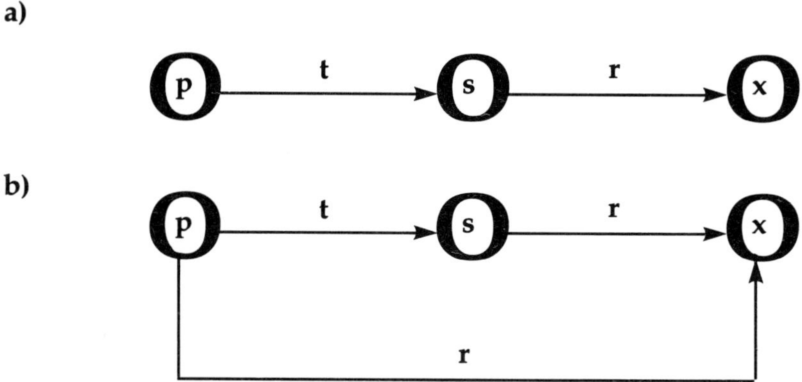

b)

Take grant graphs before and after the command:

p takes r for x from s.

Figure 3.15 Take-grant Graph Showing 'Take'

a)

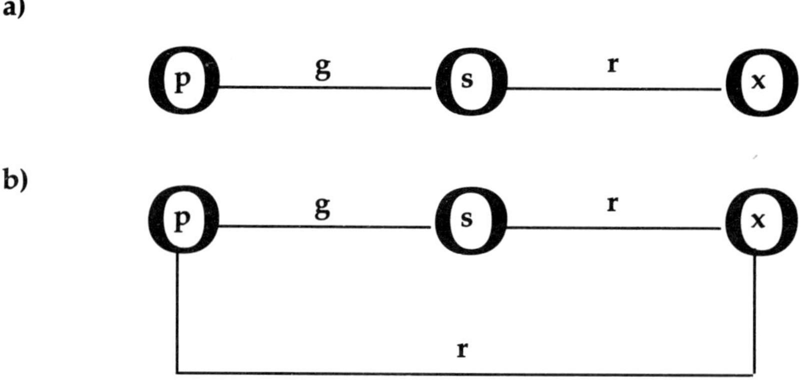

b)

Take-grant graphs before and after the command:

s grants r for x to p.

Figure 3.16 Take-grant Graph Showing 'Grant'

A fundamental theory of take-grant systems is that an initial graph G0 is unsafe in respect of s subject p acquiring right r to object x if and only if:

– There are subjects in G0 with r access to x.

– s and p are directly tg-connected.

a)

b)

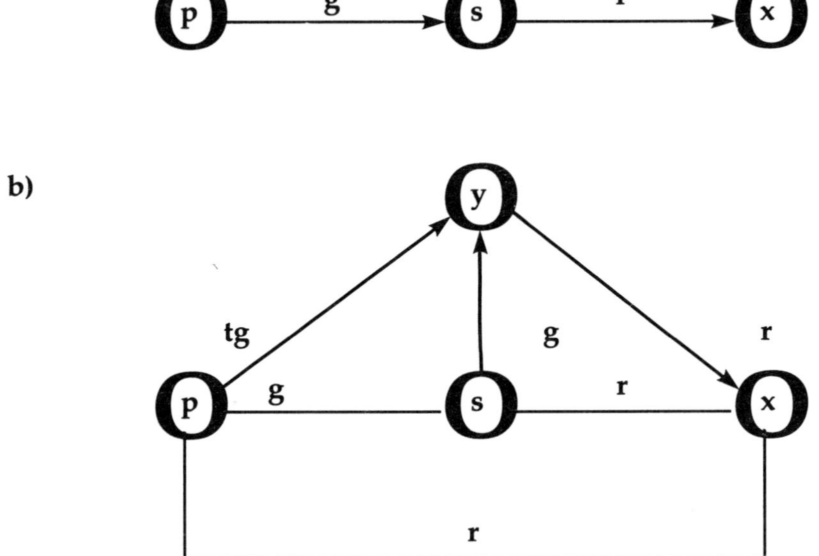

Take-grant graphs before and after the sequence of commands:

p creates tg for new object y
p grants g for y to s
s grants r for x to y
p takes r for x from y.

Figure 3.17 Take-grant Graph, Indirect Rights Acquisition (a)

This result is proven by considering each of the possible four cases that may occur, and these are shown in Figures 3.15, 3.16, 3.17 and 3.18. Intuitively, this result holds because:

1. There are no commands for adding rights to an existing arc, so at least one arc leading to the target node must already be labelled with the required right.

2. The commands for adding an arc between existing nodes require that they are already tg-connected, otherwise the rights needed to add an arc are not in place.

In the case or directly tg-connected nodes this is easy.

a)

b)

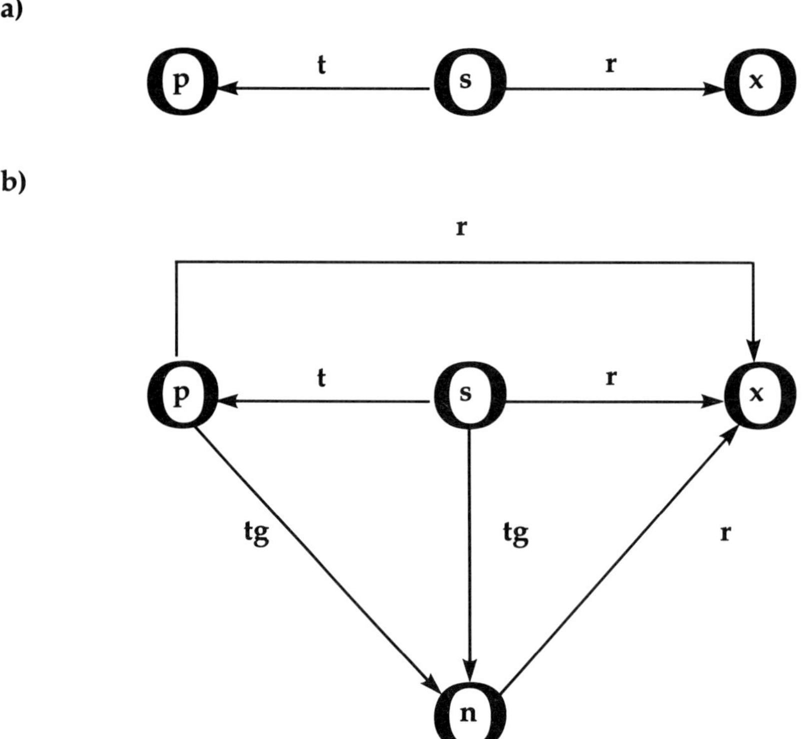

Take-grant graphs before and after the sequence of commands:

p creates tg for new object n
s takes tg for n from p
s grants r for x to n
p takes r for x from n.

Figure 3.18 Take-grant Graph, Indirect Rights Acquisition (b)

If all nodes are subjects the above holds because each node in any path may be the subject (initiator) of arc writing command. If some nodes are objects (in the sense that they are passive, excluding the possibility of subjects being a subtype of objects — an 'SO' take-grant system), then the above must be extended because object nodes cannot be the subject of a command (an object cannot 'issue' take, grant or new commands required to effect rights transfer). Objects thus provide a suitable model for protection boundaries or trusted programs, in that they can act as barriers to the transfer of rights along tg-connected paths.

3.5 SOME MATHEMATICAL FOUNDATIONS

A mathematical structure known as a lattice is frequently used in the specification of security policy models for secure operating systems. The TCSEC requires that systems above division C are capable of supporting this structure.

A lattice is not a complex structure, but has some useful properties. Essential basics of mathematical set theory are introduced to provide sufficient background to the discussions of Multi-Level Security (MLS) and information flow controls which follow.

Partially Ordered Sets

Lattices are formed from sets of objects and relations defined over them. The starting point of describing a lattice is the partially ordered set or 'poset'. A poset is a set that has three properties under an ordering relation. If the set A consists of the integers in the range 0 through 9, and the ordering relation is < (where the symbol < means 'is less than or equal to'), then the resultant structure is a poset, notated as $(A, <)$.

Three properties of a poset are illustrated in terms of this example, in which the items a, b and c are all members of the poset. A poset $(A, <)$ has the properties of:

- *Reflexivity*, $a < a$, since each member of A is less than or equal to itself.

- *Antisymmetry*, $(a < b) \wedge (b < a) \rightarrow a = b$, if a is less than or equal to b, and b is less than or equal to a, then a equals b.

  — *Transitivity, (a<b)* ∧ b< c) − > a < c, if a is less than or equal to b, and
  b is less than or equal to c, then a is less than or equal to c.

In this example, all members of the poset may be directly compared with one
another, but for many posets this is not the case. For example, if the members
of A were not integers, but sets of colours, a subset relation forming a poset
would hold between members such as {red, white} and {red, white, blue},
but members such as {red, blue} and {indigo, violet} would not be directly
comparable. It is for this reason that the set is described as being only partially
ordered, since some members may exist which are not ordered by the relation.

The subset relation

The subset relation is important in the lattice structuring applied to secure
computer systems, being used in MLS in respect of object category attributes.
It is thus important to appreciate how the properties of reflexivity,
antisymmetry and transitivity exist for a poset formed from a set of sets.

Consider the following sets:

R	=	{red}
W	=	{white}
B	=	{blue}
RW	=	{red, white}
WB	=	{white, blue} RB = {red, blue}
RWB	=	{red, white, blue}
A	=	{R,W,B,RW,WB,RB,RWB}

The set A forms a poset under the subset relation C. When we say that set
X is a subset of set Y, written X C Y, we are stating that every member of X
is also a member of Y (ie that Y contains every member of set X). This is
confirmed by checking that the necessary properties of reflexivity,
antisymmetry and transitivity hold:

(a) *Reflexivity:* R ⊂ R, ⊂{red} ⊂, ie, every member of R is a member
  of R.

(b) *Antisymmetry:* the only cases in which this can apply are those where the
  sets being related are identical.

(c) Transitivity: R⊂ RW⊂ RWB, {red} ⊂ {red, white} ⊂ {red, white, blue}.

It is clear that the subset relation does not order all the sets, for example R, W and B cannot be compared. The ordering relation may be something other than the ≤ and ⊆ relations used in the examples.

Ordered Sets

A fully ordered set, described as having a 'linear order', is one in which all members are ordered under the relation in question. The partially ordered set of integers described previously is, in fact, also a set with a 'linear order'.

Upper and Lower Bounds

Given a poset, (a set of sets), we can define upper and lower bounds of the poset. For example, in the set of integers between 0 and 9 ordered by the ⊂ relation, 0 is the lower bound and 9 is the upper bound. Note that these bounds may not be unique, since a poset is only partially ordered, for example, {red}, {white} and {blue} are all lower bounds of the set A already described.

The elements forming the sets of upper and lower bounds are themselves ordered under the poset forming relation. This gives rise to the consideration of Greatest Lower Bound and a Least Upper Bound elements, referred to as the GLB and LUB respectively. The GLB and LUB operators may be used to construct a greatest lower bound and least upper bound for any two or more given members of a set.

A Lattice is a poset in which every finite subset has a GLB and LUB. Thus the GLB and LUB operation (or relation) applies to every selection of members from the poset. The posets used in the examples, formed from the integers in the range 0 to 9 under the subsets of the set   red, white, blue   under   are both lattices.

Multi-Level Security

Multi-Level Security (MLS) policies are often modelled by a lattice structure.

The TCSEC defines MLS in terms of hierarchical 'classification' and non-hierarchical 'category' security attributes. The hierarchical attributes form a linear lattice, and the non-hierarchical attributes form a subset lattice. The ordering relation used in the TCSEC combines both the $\leq$ and $\subseteq$ relations, applied to the hierarchical classificaiton and non-hierarchic category attributes respectively.

The relation $\leq$; $\subseteq$ between objects is referred to as dominance of A by B if, and only if, B is an upper bound of A (*see* Figure 3.19). The axioms (rules) of MLS may be expressed as follows, where L is a security level and S is a set of security category labels:

- (L',S') dominates (L,S) if and only if $L \leq L'$ and $S \subset S$.

- The GLB of (L,S) and $(L'S')$ is given by $(\min (L,L'), S \cap S)$.

- The LUB of (L,S) and (L',S') is given by $(\max (L,L'), S \cup S)$.

- { } = 'system low' = (unclassified, { }).

- 'System high' = (Top secret, {categories}).[10]

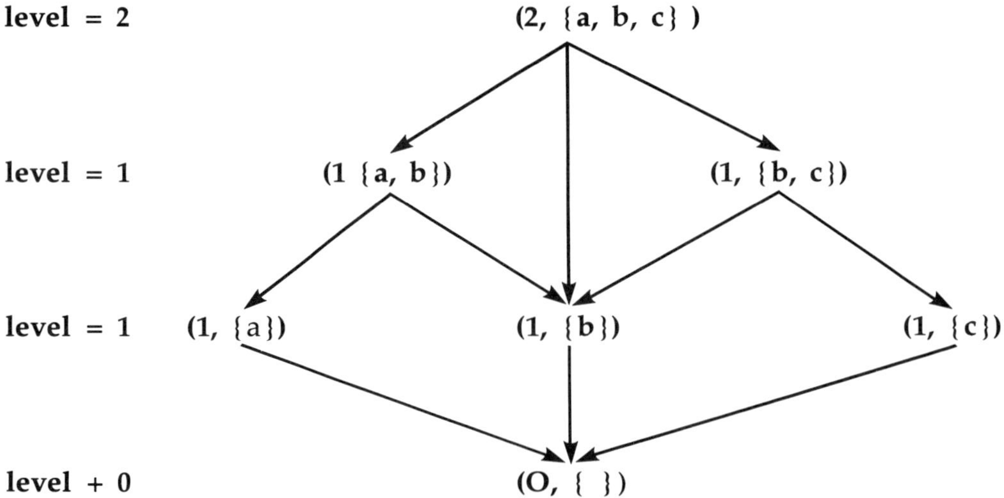

An MLS lattice structure showing dominance relations between objects of different security attributes.

Figure 3.19 An MLS Lattice Structure

Mandatory integrity policy models may also be based on lattice structures, either linear lattices (such as in the SCOMP system) or subset lattices (such as in the VME High Security Option). In the case of integrity policies, it is normally the case that subject x may read object only if the object has higher integrity than the subject, and x may write to y only if the subject has higher integrity than the object.

3.6 INFORMATION THEORY

Information theory quantifies information in units of 'bits', not to be confused with the term 'binary digits' as commonly used in respect of computer hardware.[11]

Information theory is based on mathematical probability theory and models the transfer of messages that change our perception of the probability of some event occurring (ie they provide us with additional information concerning the likeli- hood that the event will happen). To obtain the number of bits in a given event, it is first necessary to determine the probability of the event. This is then expressed as a logarithm to base 2, $I = \log_2^{(Pi)}$ where p is the probability of event i. Intuitively this is the number of binary digits needed to express the probability of an event as a binary fraction. The effect of this is that highly probable events are considered to convey only a small amount of information, while unlikely events are considered to convey a large amount of information. This is appealing because it equates to the interest generated by unexpected events. For example, if an event is certain, its probability is 1, and since $\log_2(1)=0$, no information is transferred by a message describing this event. Alternatively, if the probability of an event is 0.5, one bit of information is associated with an occurrence of this event since $\log_2(0.5)=1$. The probability of an event is often conditioned on some other event. This is measured as the conditional probability p,(j), or joint probability p(i,j) of both events occurring together.

Information theory enables information flow to be measured during the state transitions in a system, and once detected the legality of these flows in terms of security policy may be checked. To detect information flow, the system being analysed is considered in terms of each state it may assume. Assume for example, that $i=\log_2 Pa(b)$ is the probability of b given a when the system is in state i. Assume also that a given operation causes the system to undergo a state change from state i to state j, and that $j=\log_2 Pa$ (b) is the probability of b given a in this new state.

If j   i, then b (given a) is less uncertain in the new state, and this constitutes an information flow from a to b during the state transition. For example, suppose a system has two integer variables x and y. In the first system state, x has a value in the range 0 to 3 (with an equal probability for each value in this range), and y has the value x/2 (either 0 or 1, since y is an integer). In this case, given a value of y, the information in x is given by $\log_2(0.5) = 1\log2(0.5) = 1$ bit (if y is 0, then x is 0 or 1, and if y is 1 then x is either 2 or 3, in either case x has one of only two possible values with equal probability). Suppose now that the system state is changed by the operation 'x = y', with the usual meaning of assignment associated with this notation in programming languages. In this new state, the value of x is known absolutely, given the value of y, that is, * bits of information are now encoded in x. In this example, one bit of information is transferred from x to y during the system state transition.

The study of information flows in secure operating systems has primarily been in the area of flows occurring in system specifications. The flow of information between objects appearing in a specification, or variables and procedures in a program implementation, may be subject to the constraints of a security policy. This situation occurs in multi-level software, notably in security kernels and trusted software, where the flows must be verified for higher levels of the TCSEC to determine whether they represent a covert channel.

A system being analysed is considered in terms of the states it assumes, and the transitions between states caused by an operation on a given state. Each state is defined by the sensitivity of information occurring in each of its objects, and the operations correspond to statements in the system description.

For example, the statements:

        IF A: = 0 THEN B: = 1
        IF B: = 0 THEN Y: = 1

may cause an illegal flow from object A to object Y when A is not set to 1.

The information flows that may occur in a system are described as either explicit or implicit from the description statements. Explicit flows are those that occur from the direct movement of data between objects. For example, in the case of the assignment operation A: = B, information flows directly from B to

A, and an information flow policy might require that the security class of A be greater or equal to that of B.

Implicit flows occur when the value of an object is somehow dependent on some other object, although an explicit flow may not occur. In many cases the value of the former object may not absolutely disclose the value of the latter object, although it may disclose the value of the object with a probability of greater than zero. Such a relationship nevertheless represents an information flow between objects, and one that can be measured using information theory.

Implicit flows occur in a variety of subtle forms:

- In conditional statements, from the variables in the conditional expression to variables changed in the legs of the statement.

- In cycles, from the cycle counter variable to variables within the cycle body. In the case of non-terminating cycles, flow may also occur to variables outside the cycle body since these may not be reassigned as expected by statements beyond the cycle body.

- Via semaphore variables used to synchronise or order concurrent operations.

- As a result of program exceptions, such as addressing exceptions or division by zero, which might affect the value of variables elsewhere in the system.

In the case of procedure or function calls, it is required to show that the flows from all read only parameters are allowed. It is usually required that procedures do not have side-effects, in the sense that they do not access global variables.

3.7 THE BELL AND LAPADULA MODEL

The Bell and LaPadula model is probably the best known of the models of security in computing systems.[12] It was one of the earliest formal models that dealt with multi-level security, and is specifically referred to in the TCSEC criteria. The model provided a formal expression of multi-level security, which had previously only been described in informal or notional terms. It provided considerable insight into the nature and potential properties of secure systems, and provided the foundations upon which later models were based.

Security in the Bell and LaPadula model is a property deemed to exist by virtue of the following five rules being enforced:

1. The simple security property, requiring that a subject may not read from any object that has a higher classification than the subject.

2. The *-property ('star-property'), requiring that a subject may not write to an object that has a security attribute of less than the subjects level, that a subject may only read and write to an object with security attributes equal to those of the subject; and that a subject may not read from an object that has greater security attributes than those of the subject.

3. The tranquillity principle, requiring that a subject cannot alter the security attributes of any active object.

4. Non-accessibility of inactive objects, requiring that inactive objects cannot be accessed by any subject.

5. Rewriting of inactive objects, requiring that newly activated objects contain no information ('detritus') from any previous use of that object.

The Bell and LaPadula model describes an access control mechanism, enforcing security requirements when active objects (users and processes) attempt to interact with other objects, such as files and devices. Its structure is that of a mathematical lattice, which is fundamental to the Bell and LaPadula model, and to many of its derivatives and developments.

An extension to the basic model considers hierarchical structures such as those of file system directory trees. The basic requirement is that the root of the tree has a security attribute equal to the lower bound of the entire system and that the attributes of objects encountered when searching paths through the tree, should be monotonically non-decreasing in terms of their security attributes. An important implication of this is that the root may be accessed for files of any attribute. If this were not the case, it would be impossible for a process to search a directory path for a file with a lesser or equal security attribute, if the path contains an object with a greater security attribute than that of the process.

The subjects and objects in the model are labelled with a hierarchic security level and a set of security category names.

The Simple Security Property (SS-property)

The model describes the protection state of a system in terms of a set of triples, where each triple can be thought of as corresponding to an entry in an access control matrix, formed by a subject name, an object name and an access right taken from the matrix cell indexed by the subject and object in question.

A member (S,O,x) of the set, $S \times O \times A$ where S is the set of users, O is the set of objects and A is the set of access rights, is said to satisfy the simple security condition relative to f, if and only if the security level of S is greater than or equal to that of 0, and if the security category set of S includes the security category set of 0. The SS-property is a formal expression of the 'dominance' relation described in many descriptions of multi-level security.

The Basic Security Theorem

The basic security theorem states that following a system state transition, the only elements that need be checked for conforming with security, as expressed by the SS-property, are those that represent subjects whose access to objects has changed in some way. Elements of the system state, for which this is not the case, need not be considered in establishing the security of the new state, nor are states of the system that are reachable from the new state. The major importance of this theorem is that the only significant factors are the current state and the desired action upon it. This turns out to be extremely important in simplifying verification efforts in highly secure systems.

The No-Write-Down or Star Property

The No-Write-Down (NWD) property is normally referred to as the 'star-property' or *-property. It was devised following the observation that a process could read from an object at a certain level, and simultaneously write into an object at a lower level. This action could be in breach of security policy, if information from the former object were copied into the latter object.

The NWD-property and revised SS-property, taken together, constitute the total view of security under the Bell and LaPadula model.

3.8 SEPARATION KERNELS

A separation kernel is a software mechanism of minimal complexity, whose purpose is to partition a real machine architecture into several separate logical copies. To prove the adequacy of a security kernel it is necessary to demonstrate the lack of information flow between isolated virtual environments. Conventional information flow analysis does not provide an ideal technique for achieving this, since security kernel primitives, such as the swap operation, involve accessing state variables from the originating environment and from some other environment, while the objective is actually to demonstrate the lack of interaction between environments. For a separation kernel, specification complexity should be minimal, and directly related to the architecture, so that verification becomes minimally difficult. The verification objective for a separation kernel is to prove that the virtual environment is indistinguishable from the real environment and that isolated virtual environments do not interact in any way. This is called 'proof of separability'.

Notes:

1   Jar 86a, Gra 82a
2   Sal 75a, p1302
3   Lam 74a, Gra 72a, Har 76a
4   Lam 74a
5   Gra 72a
6   Gra 72a
7   ANS 87a
8   Jon 76a, Den 82a
9   Jon 76a
10 Den 82a
11 Sha 48a
12 Bel 77a

(*see* Reference section).

4   Protection mechanisms

4.1   INTRODUCTION

Protection mechanisms are the primary means of ensuring separation between objects in a system and they may be classified as being active or passive.

Active protection mechanisms prevent access to some object if the access is not known to the protection mechanism as being authorised. An example of such a mechanism is memory protection as provided by many computer hardware architectures, where access to objects at certain addresses may be controlled depending on such criteria as the current processor state and attributes of the process attempting to reference the object in question.

Passive protection mechanisms are those that prevent or detect unauthorised use of the information associated with an object, even if access to the object itself is not prevented. Typically, these techniques are based on cryptographic secrecy techniques to prevent unauthorised disclosure of information, or on cryptographic and checksum techniques to detect unauthorised alteration of an object.

There is often an ultimate dependency on physical security to protect the devices implementing protection mechanisms, for example to prevent addressing hardware from being incapacitated or encryption keys from being referenced from outside a cryptographic unit (however, issues of physical security are not considered further here).

Protection mechanisms are often implemented in hardware or microcode, and control access to primitive objects such as memory, machine code instructions and registers (including those used to control I/O operations).

4.2 PROCESSOR PRIVILEGE STATES

A common concept is for the architecture to support two states of processor privilege for protecting sensitive instructions.[1] The principle concerned is to record the processor state in a register that can only be altered when the processor is operating in the privileged state. Sensitive instructions (such as initiating I/O or disabling the interrupt mechanism) are implemented to include reference to the register and the instruction is aborted if privileged state is expected but not current.

Entry into privileged mode is typically controlled by the hardware and microcode when handling of certain types of interrupt. One or more interrupts will be defined as system calls, and these can be caused by code running in non-privileged mode to invoke the functions of privileged operating system routines. When an interrupt is detected, the hardware saves the current processor state, and enters a first-level interrupt handler (normally in privileged mode). Parameters to and from system calls are commonly passed by storing data or references to data (addresses) in designated registers or at predetermined addresses in memory. Protection schemes can be used to protect operating systems from untrusted user code, and one possible definition of an operating system on such a machine is that the operating system is that software which runs in privileged mode.[2] Such schemes are fundamental in many contemporary systems, from mainframes such as IBM's S370 range, through to systems based on microprocessors, such as the Intel 80286 in 'protected mode'.

Such mechanisms depend upon microcode or hardware support, but certain critical elements of the overall system are inevitably implemented in software, such as parts of the interrupt handlers and those parts of the operating system that run in privileged mode. Memory protection is therefore required to protect any such elements from unauthorised change. Secure operating systems require the provision of a binary privilege state architecture as a minimum.

4.3 MEMORY PROTECTION

Memory protection is concerned with controlling access to a shared main memory. It is necessary to partition memory in such a way as to ensure that processes cannot interfere with each other's local memory and to ensure that common areas of memory are protected against unauthorised access. In particular, the memory used by the operating system must be protected to ensure that the integrity of privileged code and data is maintained (for example, to protect the data item that describes the privilege level of a process when the process is queued awaiting despatch). Memory protection is closely related to issues of addressing, and many schemes protect memory by placing it outside the address space available to a process.

Descriptor Registers

Descriptor registers provide a simple mechanism for partitioning memory.[3] A descriptor register in a simple scheme may be a protected register (ie addressable only in privileged mode) used to contain addressing base and limit values (*see* Figure 4.1). The base and limit values are used as part of the addressing scheme, such that a program cannot use addresses greater than the 'limit' value. The 'base' value is added to all addresses before they are passed to the memory controller (ie it becomes the lowest address available to the current code).

The addresses used by a program are not the physical addresses recognised by hardware unless the 'base'value is zero. Therefore, it is possible to define a set of (base, limit) pairs in such a way that access to sensitive areas of memory is controlled and non-privileged code procedures access disjoint areas of physical memory. It would normally be a responsibility of privileged operating system routines to maintain a list of descriptor register values associated with each process and to load these into the descriptor registers prior to passing control to non-privileged processes. The privileged routines themselves may run with all physical addresses accessible.

Further flexibility may be added to the scheme by increasing the number of descriptor registers available (see figure 4.2). Different base/limit values may be loaded into each register and if addressing values or fields within instructions are used to select the appropriate descriptor register, controlled access to a non-contiguous range of physical addresses can be provided without the need to reload descriptor registers. This allows code and data to be accessed from different areas of memory, plus the definition of shared memory areas available to a number of processes.

Increasing the number of immediately accessible blocks of memory introduces a requirement for improved control over the type of access available to different addressable areas of memory.

Example of the use of base and limit registers, constraining memory access to addresses in the range 1000-2000.

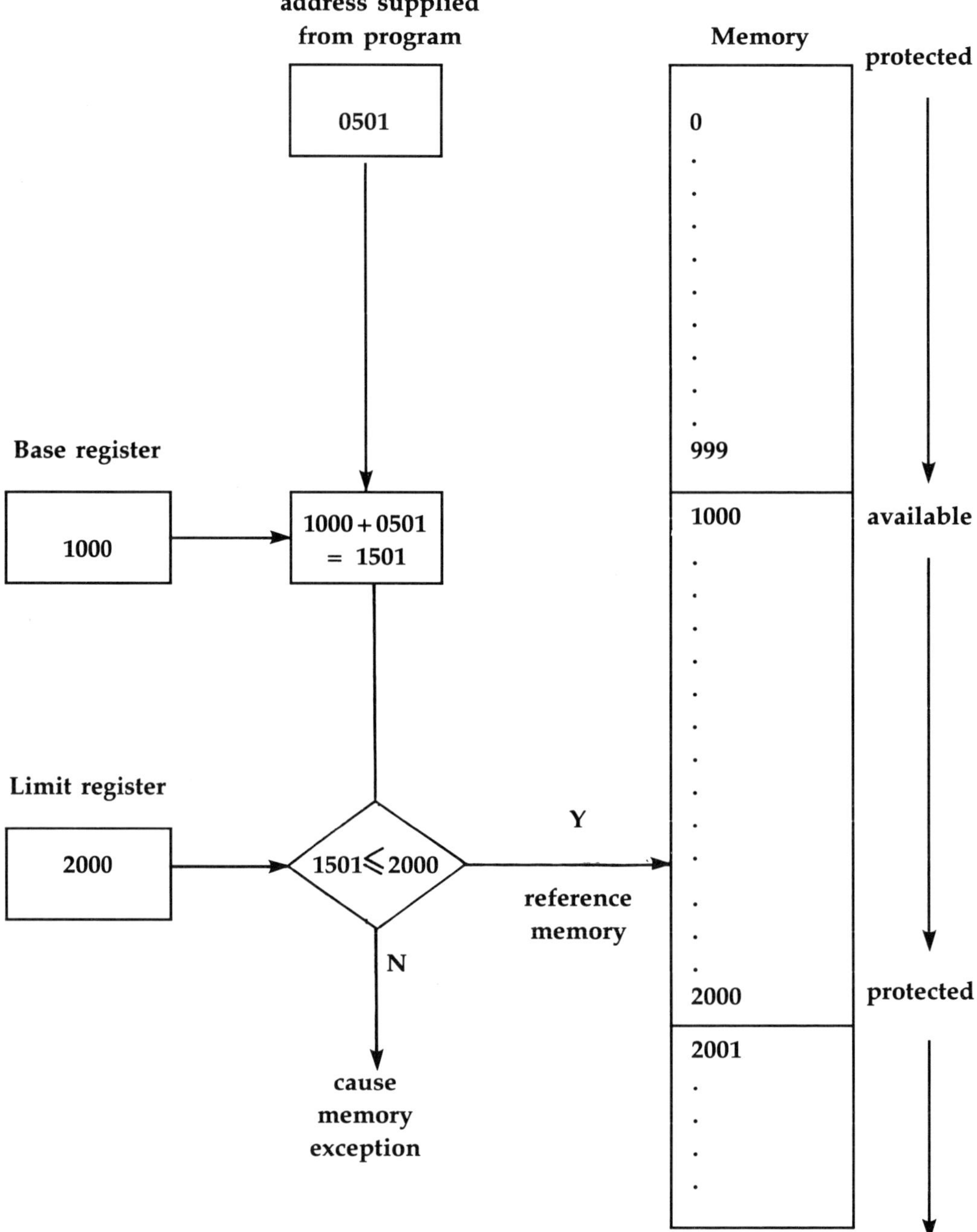

Figure 4.1 Base and Limit Registers

Use of multiple base and limit registers to partition memory.

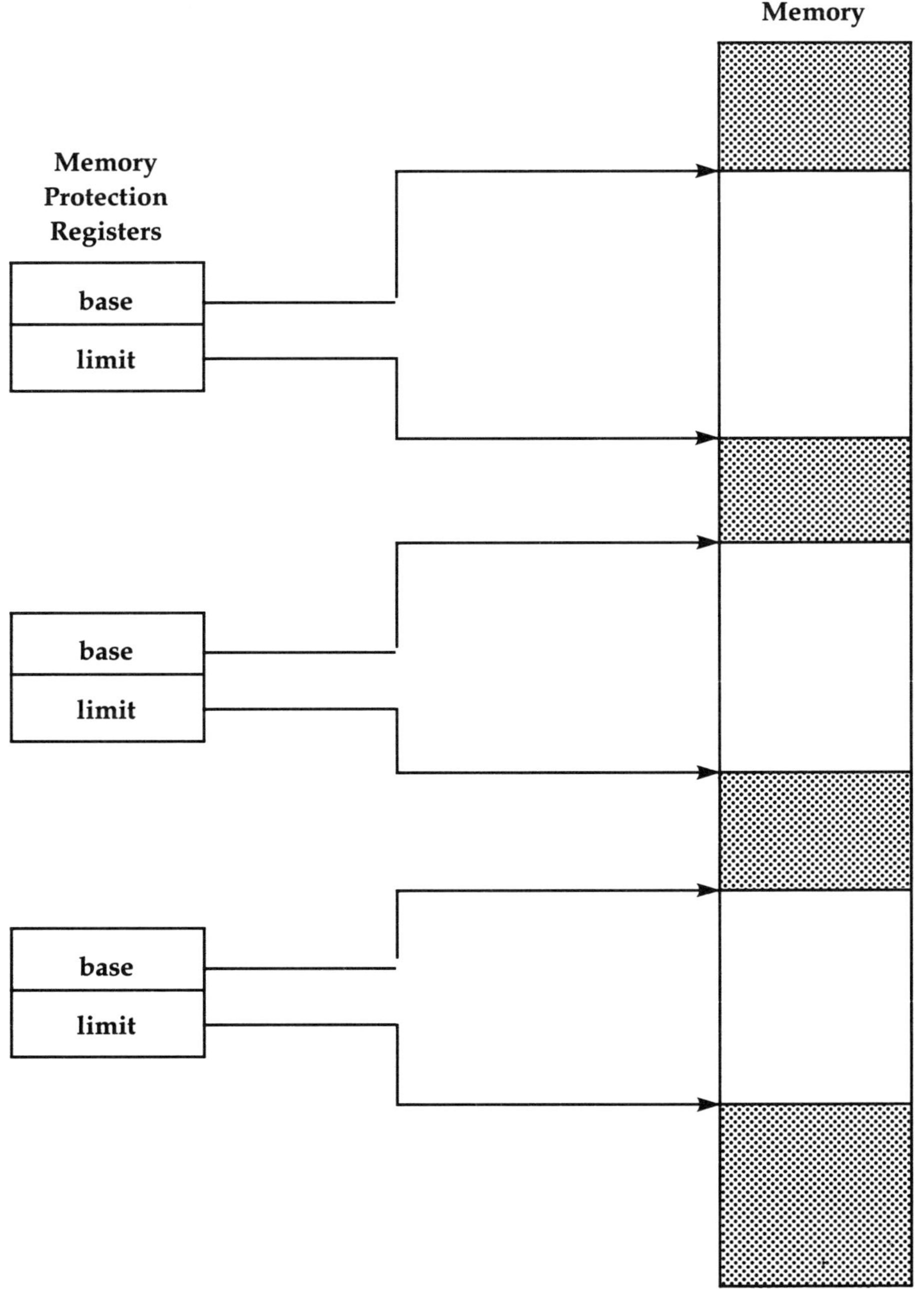

Figure 4.2 Multiple Base and Limit Registers

It becomes important, for example, to be able to prevent code or read-only areas from being overwritten, resulting in the need to associate protection information with areas of memory.

Segmentation

Segmentation is a technique that partitions an address space, allowing different partitions (segments) to have different access attributes. The following definition is useful:

> "A segment is a set of words whose addresses are contiguous in
> a virtual address space, and whose protection status is at all times
> the same." *(Needham R M, 1972)*.

As with the basic bounds and limit mechanisms, this discussion is limited to the effects of segmentation on security. Other useful attributes of segment-ation, such as relocatability of code and data areas are not the concern here.

It should be apparent that this is a natural extension of partitioned memory, using base and limit techniques (*see* Figure 4.3). It should also be clear that it excludes those schemes commonly known as 'segmented memory', that are used on contemporary micro processors to extend the range of addressable memory locations by using a 'segment register' and calculating memory accesses relative to an n-byte block of words, referenced by the segment register. Such schemes overcome addressing limitations, but do not usually have useful security properties, ie segments may often overlap and the segment register is often unprotected in these schemes.

Many implementations of segmented memory systems allow attributes, other than those concerned with protection, to be associated with segments. For example, an attribute may indicate that a segment is not to be relocated in memory, perhaps because it is the target for an asynchronous I/O operation. Such attributes can have a direct bearing on the correctness of system implementation.

Segmented memory systems

Segmented memory systems vary in the use they make of segment tables. The basic concept tends to be that memory addresses are mapped from the virtual

A single segment table mechanism, accessed and partitioned by a set of descriptor registers.

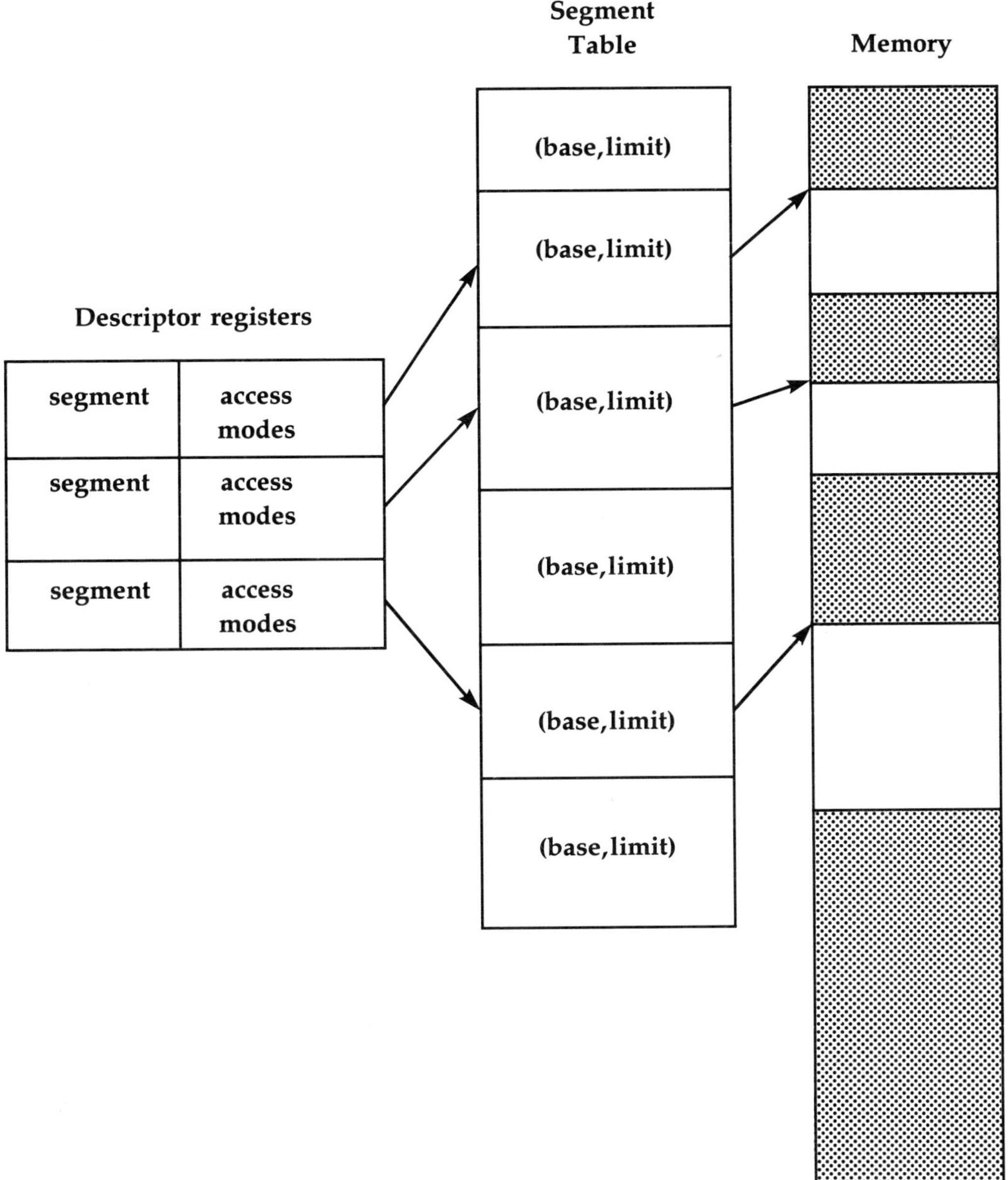

Figure 4.3 Single Segment Table

addresses known by processes, onto a set of real addresses known to hardware via segment table entries, provided that protection constraints are observed.

For reasons of efficiency, the organisation of protection data in segmented memory schemes is normally a combination of one or more of the Access Control List's capability and lock-key schemes.

A segmented memory scheme, with addresses containing a segment number and an offset within the segment.

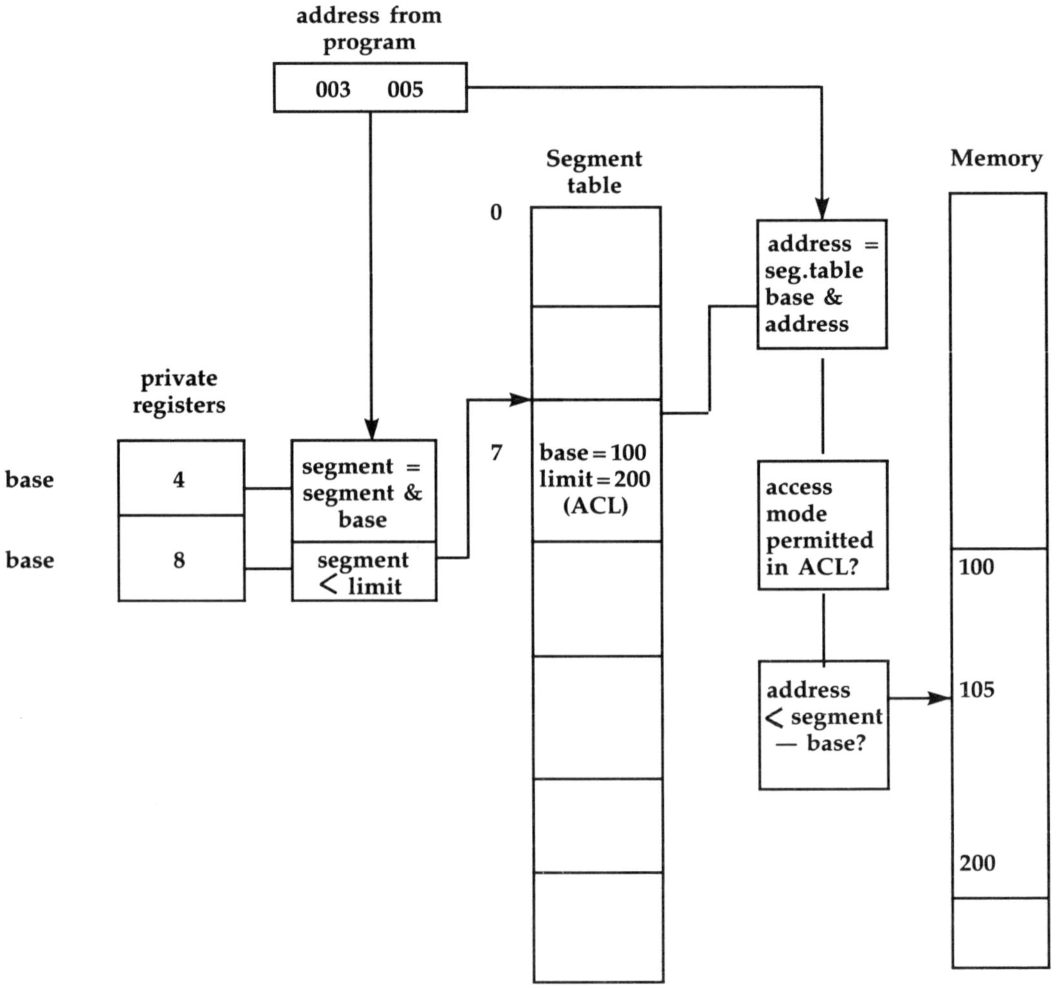

Figure 4.4 Segmented Memory

A straightforward scheme uses a single segment table directly referenced from all processes (*see* Figure 4.4). Locations in memory have the same virtual address in all processes, ie there is only a single address space. Such a scheme has the advantage of consistent addressing when shared segments are involved, since an object in a shared segment will have the same address in all processes.

Issues of protection are distanced from those of addressing as all segments are addressable in every protection domain. Protection is typically achieved by protected descriptor registers (or capability registers) loaded from a segment table entry and then used to partition the segment table. Other segmented memory schemes closely associate issues of addressing and protection.

As an example, schemes that provide a different segment table for each address space allow shared segments to be known by different names, because each local segment table may reference the segment using a different address (*see* Figure 4.5). Such schemes typically use a protected descriptor register to locate the start of the current segment table. The segments appearing within a local segment table may be a subset of the segments within the system, and provided that local segment tables are protected and the addressing mechanism cannot be circumvented, then segments which do not appear in the segment table cannot be accessed. The fact that a segment can be addressed by a number of different names can introduce problems when the segment appears in different address spaces. In particular, addresses (such as pointers) appearing within the segment may be invalid in some of the address spaces accessing the segment.[4] Approaches using indirection tables or absolute addresses for access to shared segments may be used to overcome some of these problems.[5]

Segmentation and Paging

Segmentation and paging are distinct issues under our definition of segmentation. Paging is essentially an implementation technique. It is not part of the architecture and should be transparent to processes. Moreover, paging is not a protection mechanism. Its security implications are typically limited to the potential covert channel occurring in the paging mechanism. Paging has implications for performance and address space size, in that the limitations of physical memory do not ultimately constrain the size of address space that can be supported.

Multiple segment tables, providing partitioning of memory and separation of virtual address spaces.

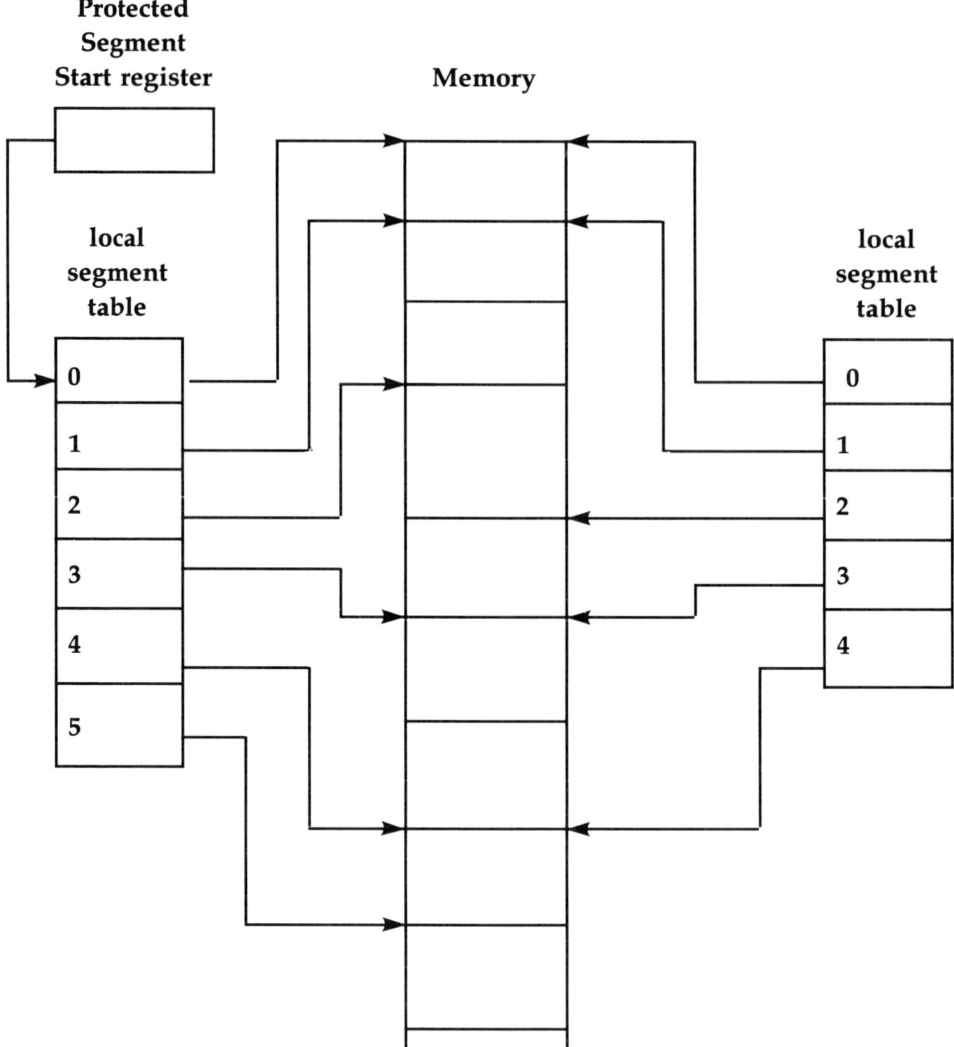

Figure 4.5 Multiple Segment Tables

In the event that an implementation combines segmentation and paging mechanisms, the paging aspects can often be ignored when considering issues of security. Such systems typically extend a paging mechanism to include protection information, possibly as a result of extending an earlier architecture. It is likely that the definition of many segments of equivalent protection status will result, since each segment is bound by the page size. Such a situation may result in a system that is more difficult to verify, but is consistent with the definition of segmentation given earlier, in that pages and segments become equivalent. As an example, the IBM System 370 architecture associates protection information with physical page frames.

Capability Based Segmentation

The descriptor register scheme previously described, supporting simple segmented memory management bears a close resemblance to a capability scheme, ie the descriptor contains an object (segment) identity and authorisation data. The use of capabilities to control access to segments thus appears to be a natural extension of this concept.

The definition of segmentation already given allows for a large number of segments of arbitrary size. In consequence, it allows for schemes where each logical object representation is stored in a separate segment. Note that this approach avoids the problems of having to move an object between segments if its protection status changes and it is sharing a segment with other objects. In such schemes the one-to-one mapping between objects and segments implies that they are effectively equivalent for protection purposes, hence the discussion of segmentation is extended to include capability addressing schemes that do not explicitly refer to the concepts of segmentation.

An important point is the role of indirection in providing protection, by associating addressing and protection issues.[6] Indirection has benefits other than protection, such as ease of handling segment relocation and deletion.

Capability based memory protection

Capability based memory protection schemes are constrained by the supporting architecture which, in the case of a tagged architecture, allows capabilities to be identified by the hardware wherever they occur; typically by a bit set by the hardware. A tagged architecture allows the construction of highly flexible and efficient capability addressing schemes, since capabilities may then be stored wherever it is most convenient, for example as integral pointers between data objects occurring in different segments. In particular, loading a capability (descriptor) register becomes a non-privileged operation, since the architecture ensures that only valid capabilities may be loaded, thus preventing unauthorised creation or modification of capabilities.

Note that unauthorised access to capabilities is prevented by the addressing mechanism, such that the memory protection mechanism is dependent upon itself (plus the architectural primitives) for its own protection. Hardware support for capabilities is rare, so it is common to devise capability schemes where capabilities are objects to be protected by the memory protection scheme rather than receiving direct support from the architecture. Under such schemes, capabilities cannot occur anywhere in memory since they become susceptible to unauthorised alteration and are thus only considered valid when loaded from 'C-lists'(equating to protected capability segments).

Multi-state Architectures

Multi-state architectures provide support for several privilege states, and as such are often referred to as being 'layered' or 'ring' structured. An ordering relation normally exists between the protection states in a multi-state system such that level n is more privileged than level n + 1. Binary protection state architectures on the other hand, partition the possible state space for a machine into two modes, ie privileged and non-privileged.

The number of levels supported in a multi-state architecture tends to vary between 4 and 16, with the current level typically being identified by a multi-bit integer field in a protected process state word. Such ordering is normally applied to system calls between levels and references to segments created at different levels.

The segments in such schemes usually include protection data identifying the privilege levels at which they are available. The current protection level of a process is changed as part of the mechanism for calling a procedure object resident in a segment, at a different protection level from that of the caller. Such segments may include data to indicate the range of protection levels from which calls may be made to procedural objects held in the segment, indicating the valid entry points (gates) into the segment (so that entry to arbitrary addresses is prohibited, and integrity related operations such as parameter validation cannot be circumvented). The mechanisms supporting ICL's VME operating system are a good example of this type of design.

Parameter Passing and Domain Switching

Calls between procedures often result in protection domain switches, so protection systems are intimately concerned with procedure call and return mechanisms. In essence the target procedure is considered as a protected object, and domain switching amounts to changing the current protection domain identifier or changing the current capability list (depending on whether access control list or capability schemes are employed). Calls that involve protection domain switching introduce problems relating to parameters passed between the procedural objects in the respective domains. Parameters passed by value do not pose problems,[7] but problems may occur whenever indirect references to segment names are passed between domains.[8]

The problem is that parameters passed by reference must point to objects available in both domains. Thus a call may pass parameters referencing objects that cannot be accessed from the target domain, so that the call may succeed but the operation of the called procedure fail when attempting to access the object (*see* Figure 4.6). More importantly, parameters may be passed that reference objects available to the called procedure which are not available within the calling procedure. If the called procedure is unable to detect this, it may retrieve or modify objects on behalf of the caller in an unauthorised fashion (*see* Figure 4.7).

Such possibilities are a major concern since loss of security results have been successfully exploited in operating system penetration exercises. The operation of validating reference parameters may need to be atomic, that is to execute to completion without interruption. This prevents the subversion of the validation sequence by processes (possibly a reactivation of the caller caused by interrupt or trap operations) whose operation is interleaved with that of the called process.[9] Even then, there exists the possibility that addresses may be changed by concurrent (or interleaved) activity in the callers domain, subsequent to validation by the called procedure but before final use of the addresses by the called procedure.[10]

Such problems may be alleviated by copying all referenced and indirect objects into the target domain prior to parameter validation. This technique is also applicable when passing parameters into 'less privileged' domains.[11] Strictly speaking, it may be necessary to perform this for all objects, indirectly referenced from the called domain, possibly involving entire linked structures of which the precise elements of interest may not be known in advance. Further, it is necessary to exclude other accesses to the referenced segments in order to prevent race conditions.

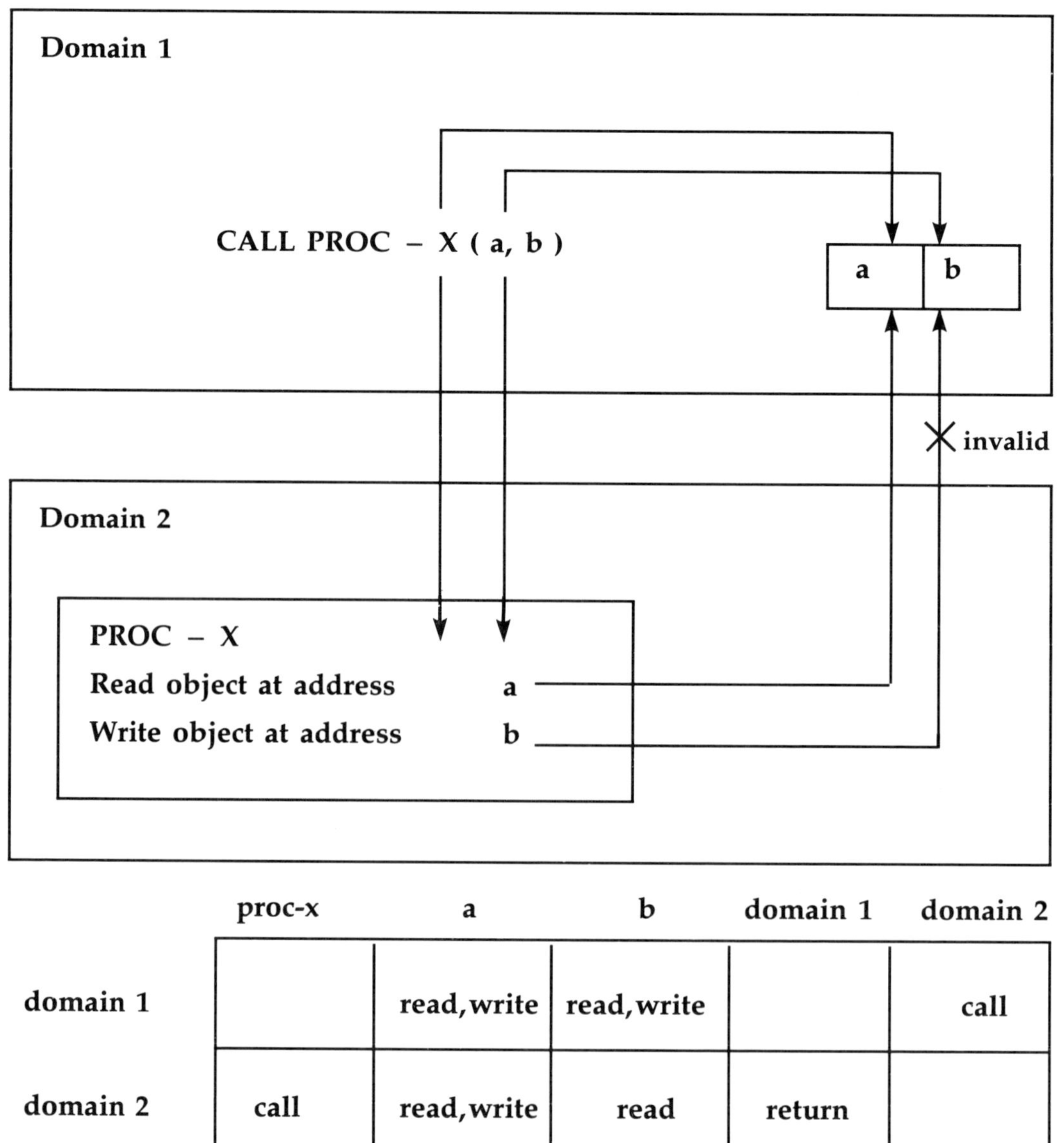

	proc-x	a	b	domain 1	domain 2
domain 1		read, write	read, write		call
domain 2	call	read, write	read	return	

Proc-x is called receiving the addresses of two objects in domain 1. References to the object at address b are not permitted in domain 2, as indicated by the access matrix.

Figure 4.6 Parameter Passing Between Protection Domains

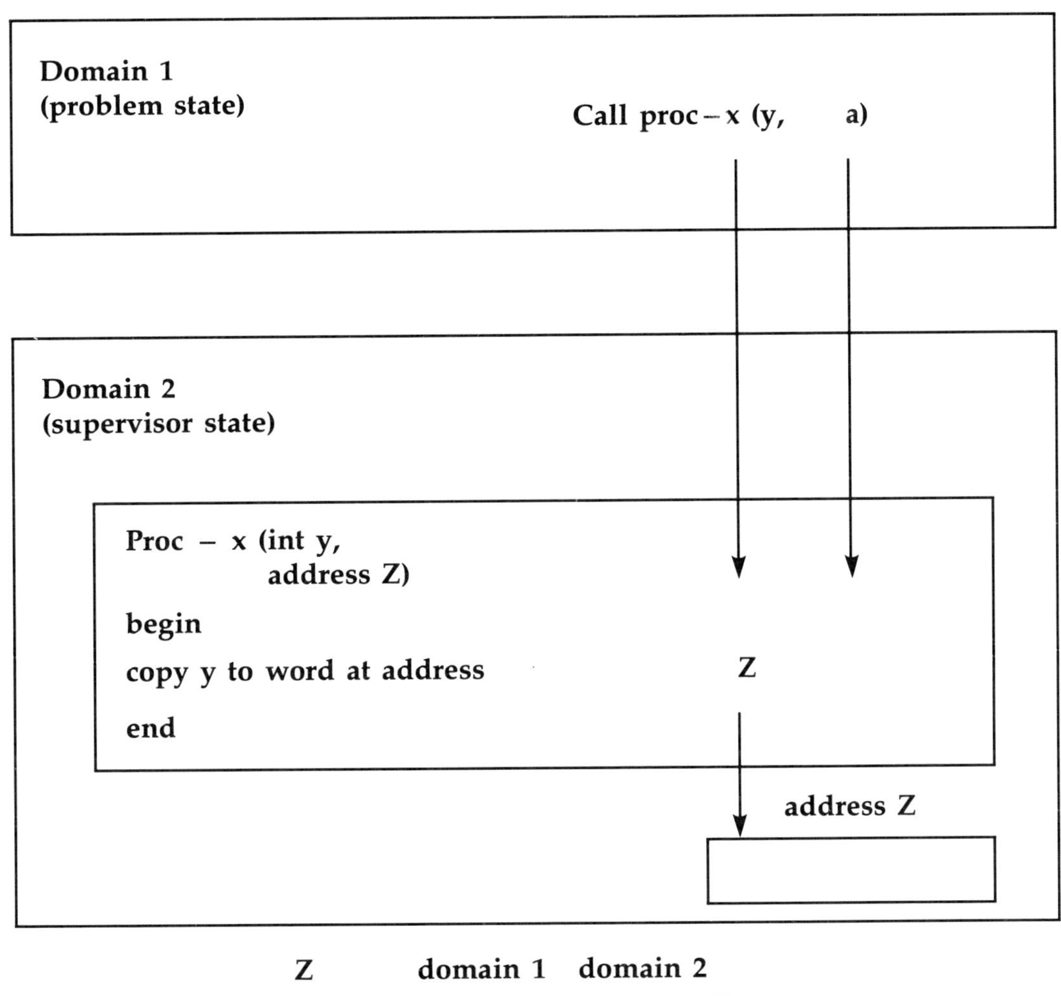

	Z	domain 1	domain 2
domain 1	read		call
domain 2	read, write	return	

Unauthorised access to an object in another protection domain, via call to an object in that domain and the use of indirect addressing. In effect, domain 1 has acquired write access to the object address Z.

Figure 4.7 Unauthorised Access between Protection Domains

Protected Subsystems

Primitive protection mechanisms are limited in terms of the support they offer for complex or abstract protection requirements. It may be necessary to handle more complex abstract objects with more sophisticated security reuirements (such as time-dependent, data-dependent, context-dependent or history-dependent conditions).

The construction of protected subsystems allows such requirements to be met. Primitive protection mechanisms are used to 'encapsulate' a set of data objects and procedure objects, so that the contents of the protected subsystem domain cannot be directly accessed from elsewhere (*see* Figure 4.8).[12] A number of entry points to procedures within the protected subsystem may be exported from the protected subsystem, with primitive protection mechanisms used to control access to these entry points, which may enforce arbitrary operations and authorisation decisions. Layered and segmented architectures facilitate such an approach, limited by the size and number of segments supported and the efficiency of the protection mechanisms. (Note that the TCSEC is referring to such designs when it refers to layering and data hiding.)

4.4 TRUSTED NETWORK INTERFACE UNITS

Trusted Network Interface Units (TNIUs) are often used in secure distributed (or networked) operating systems. TNIUs are used to provide an access point for a potentially untrusted client or server onto the communication medium supporting a distributed system (*see* Figure 4.9). This provides an opportunity to allow use of untrusted nodes, and is of major significance since it allows the use of the many microprocessor based nodes that do not provide protection mechanisms in their architecture and which may not be trusted to be memory-less (ie not to retain information for subsequent unauthorised disclosure). TNIUs also provide a suitable environment in which to implement and enforce protection of messages over a potentially untrusted communication service, using techniques of encryption and communication protocols. TNIUs may be constructed at relatively low cost (using microprocessor technology) and housed in a tamper-resistant casing. The cost per device will be dependent on the complexity of the functions implemented within the TNIU and the required performance characteristics (dictated by the throughput required of the TNIU and the bandwidth of its communication interfaces).

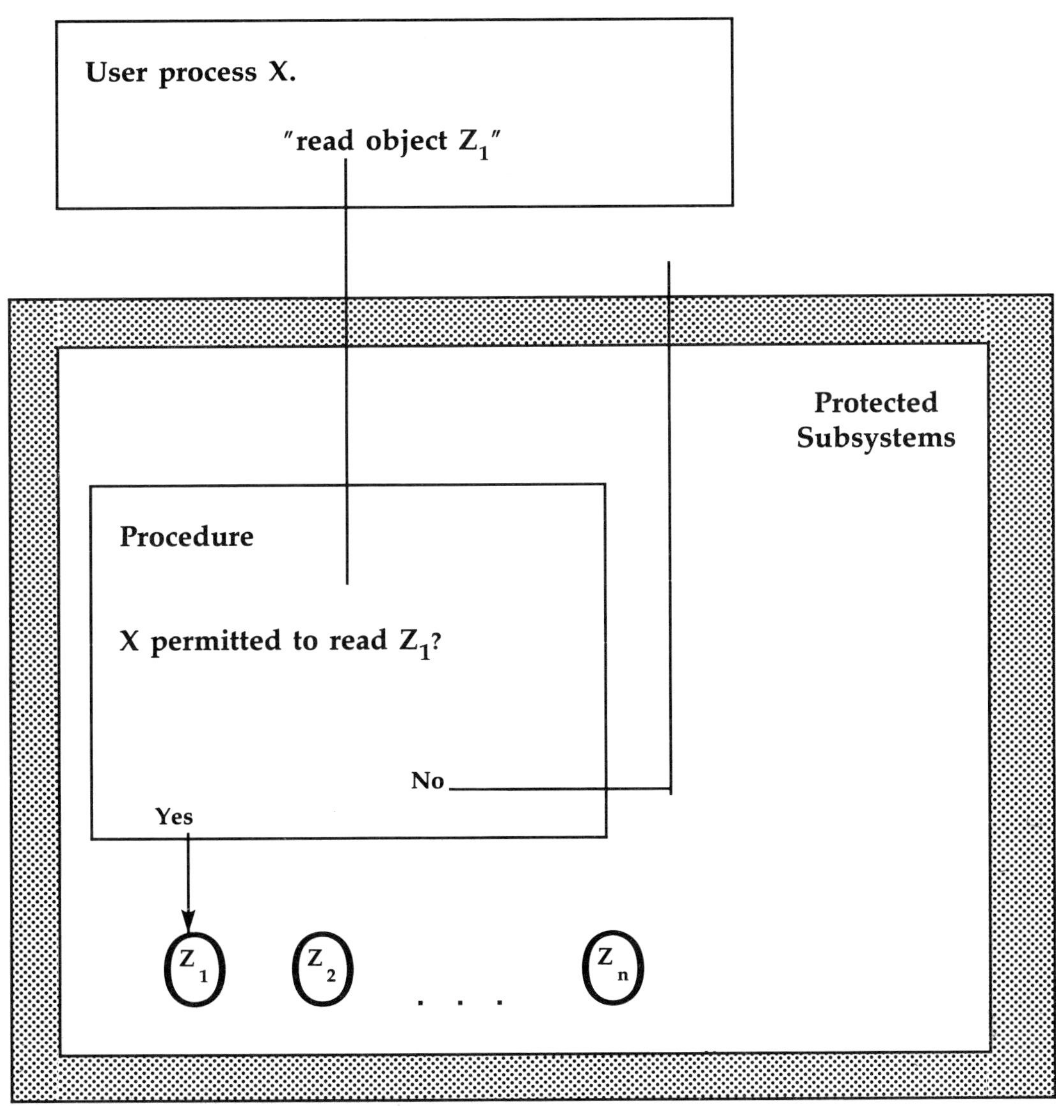

A protected subsystem managing objects of type Z. A single procedure provides the only external entry point into the protected subsystem.

Figure 4.8 Protected Subsystem

4.5 PROTECTION MECHANISM DESIGN

The implementation of a protection system must address the following issues:

- Representation of the protection information;[13]

- The need to ensure that all access attempts are subject to authorisation;[14]

- The need for appropriate methods of modifying the protection information;[15]

- The mechanics and implications of protection domain switching.[16]

Mechanisms employed for interpreting protection information were described in early works as monitors,[17] access controllers,[18] and evaluation programs. In terms of the TCSEC, the mechanism concerned would be described as a reference validation mechanism or a TCB.

The implementation of a protection mechanism does not normally model an access matrix since the inefficiency of maintaining and searching such a

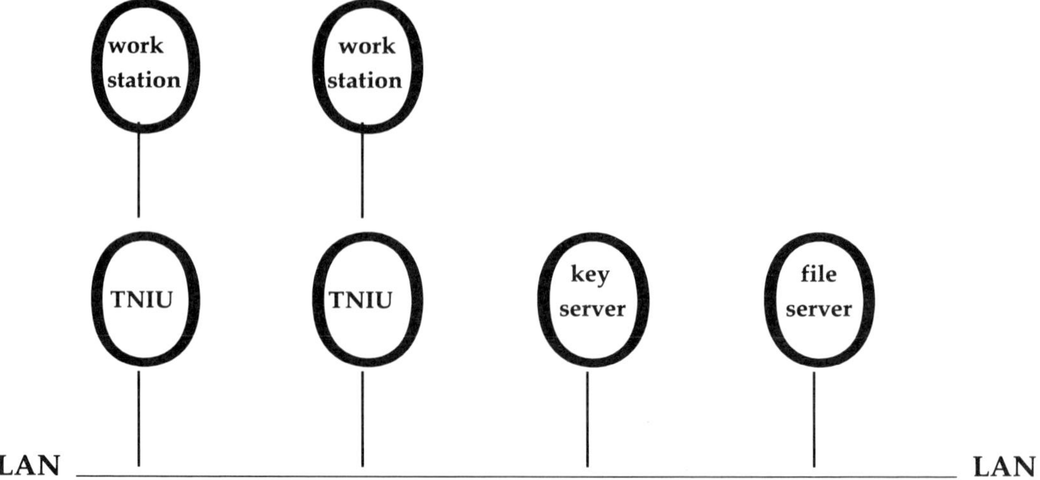

The PROSP system uses Trusted Network Interface Units to perform file and encryption key recovery by (attempting) to decrypt items recovered from the file server and key server.

Figure 4.9 TNIUs in the PROSP System

structure would often be unacceptable. Protection mechanisms are thus normally designed along one of three lines; access control lists, capability lists and lock and key schemes.[19]

Lock and Key Mechanisms

Lock and key mechanisms operate by associating a (object-name key) pair with a subject, and a list of (key, access right) pairs with each object being protected (*see* Figure 4.10). When a subject requires access to an object, it presents its (object-name, key) pair to the protection mechanism. The protection mechanism compares the supplied key and access mode against the entries in the object's (key, access right) pairs list, allowing access if a match is found. A number of entries in the object's list may be equivalent in terms of access rights with different domains obtaining equivalent access using different keys.

Lock and key systems separate issues of addressing and protection, since the protection data, ie the key, is separate from object addresses (or names). An example of a lock and key mechanism is the memory management scheme used on IBM System 370 architecture mainframes.

Access Control Lists

Access Control List (ACL) mechanisms implement vertical columns of the access matrix model for a given object (*see* Figure 4.11). An object protected under an ACL scheme has a list of (domain, right) pairs associated with it, ie enforcement checking amounts to inspection of the ACL associated with the target object seeking the name of the requesting domain and the mode of access (*see* Figure 4.12). ACL mechanisms have the advantage of performing name-protection binding at the last possible moment, ie at the time access is requested.[20]

Performing name-protection binding at access time has advantages in that it enables better control of changes to the authorisation state. If access rights are changed between access requests, the enforcement mechanism will implement the changed authorisation requirements at no additional cost. An important instance of changed authorisation state concerns revocation of access rights, which is easily performed for any object by modifying its ACL.[21] The less likely event of subject deletion is handled less efficiently, so requiring the deletion of the corresponding (subject, access) pairs from all ACLs in which they occur. This may require the scanning of every ACL in the system or the use of periodic garbage collection schemes. Similarly, auditing of ACLs is easy when determining which subjects may access a given object, but not easy if determining which object a given subject may access. The attribute of ACLs enabling close control over authorisation state changes carries an associated performance overhead. The cost of scanning ACLs can become excessive, particularly if ACL lists are long, or if subjects require to make large numbers of accesses in sequence. As an example, serial disk file processing would take considerably longer than

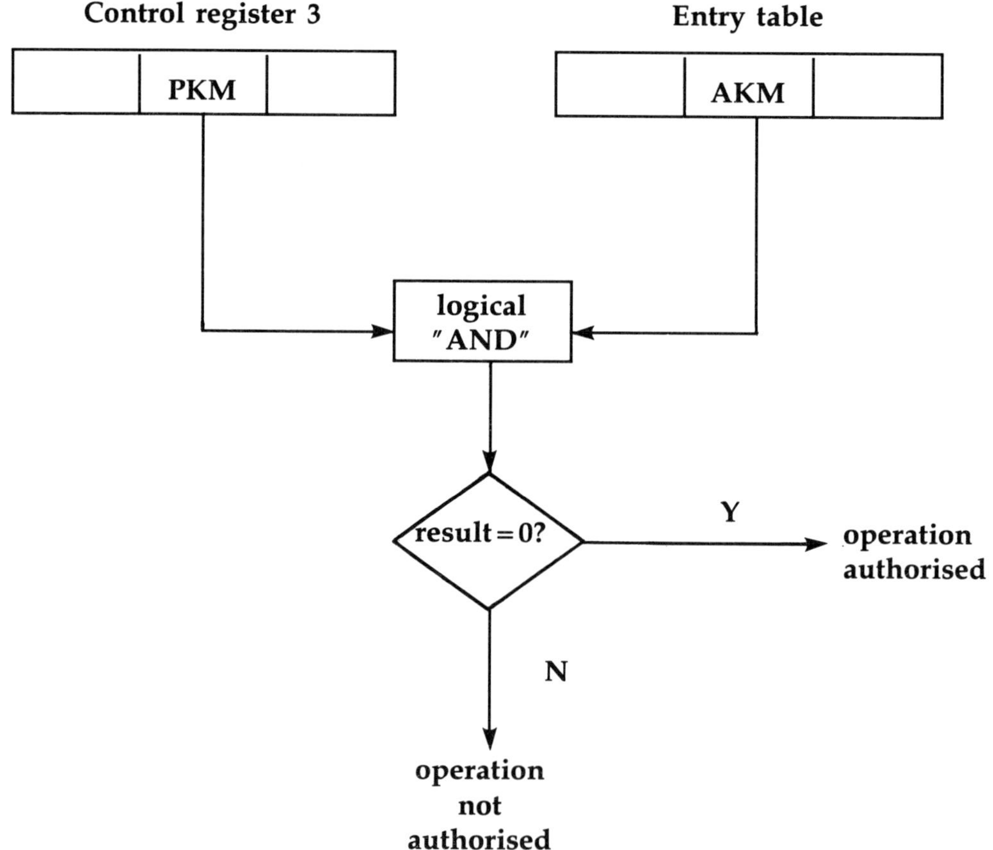

Example of a lock and key protection mechanism. Program calls using the PC instruction across address space boundaries on the IBM System 370 Extended Architecture are controlled by fields in a protected register and a protected linkage table entry.

Figure 4.10 Example Lock and Key Mechanism

usual if each request to read a record was validated against the file access permissions maintained by the file system. Access control of memory and registers demands even greater efficiency.

When efficient operation or simplicity of design is required, the costs of ACL evaluation may be limited by placing bounds on the number of entries in the ACL. A common example of this approach exists in file systems on small

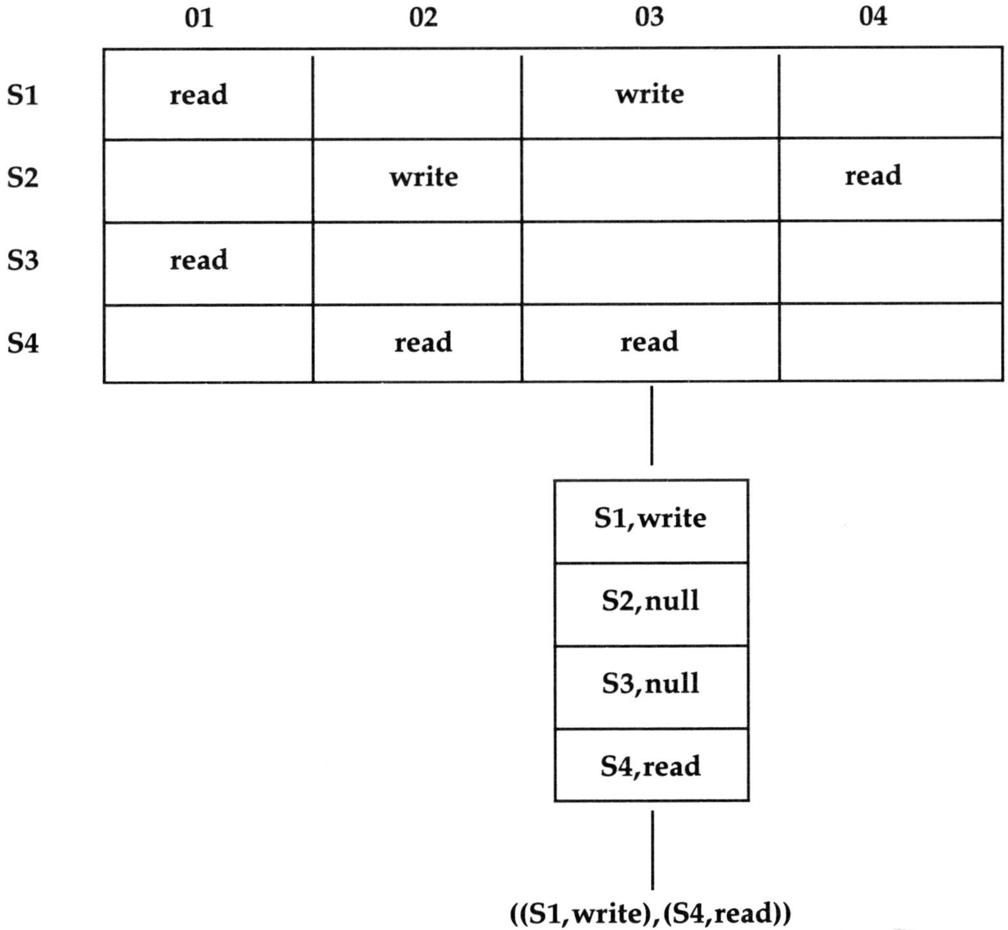

An access control list may be derived from a column within an access control matrix, but will not normally be a direct representation for reasons of efficiency in the case of large matrices.

Figure 4.11 Access Control List

computer operating systems. Rather than represent permissions to all possible subjects in ACLs, it is common in such systems to have permission controls over the object owner, a group of users and the total set of users. When such a scheme is adopted, ACL entries can be efficiently encoded as a sequence of bit fields, where each field is associated with a (set of) subject(s), and each bit within a field indicates a particular type of access mode (read, write, etc).

Capability Based Mechanisms

Capability based protection mechanisms implement the horizontal row of an access matrix model corresponding to a given subject. For each object, a (object, rights) pair is termed a 'capability' (*see* Figure 4.13). For access to be authorised to a protected object, the requesting subject must be in possession of an appropriate capability for that object. The possession of capabilities confers privilege, so it is essential that capabilities must not be forgeable or corruptible, otherwise they could be generated or altered to obtain unauthorised access permissions. Therefore, capabilities are objects that require protection.

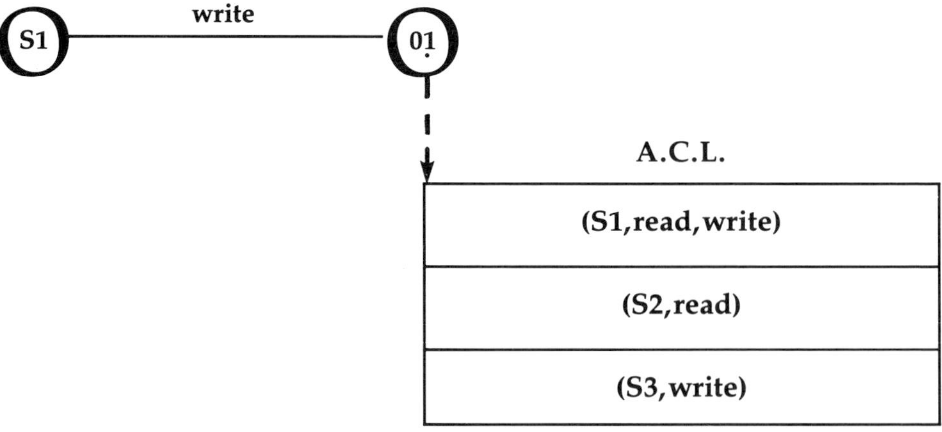

Access by S1 to 01 is authorised if the access control list associated with O1 contains an entry for S1 with the relevant access mode.

Figure 4.12 Conceptual Access Control List

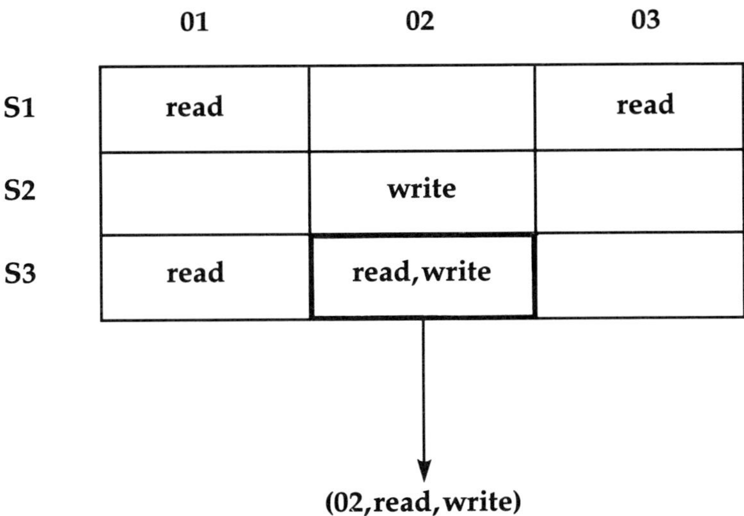

Correspondence between access matrix cells and capabilities.

Figure 4.13 Access Matrix Cells and Capabilities

Tagging

Capabilities may be protected using special hardware techniques known as 'tagging', in which storage locations holding capabilities are tagged by an unaddressable field which indicates that the location contains a capability.[22]

The majority of contemporary architectures do not provide support tagging. A practical approach for protecting capabilities is to store them in protected areas of memory, often called 'capability-segments', and to control their availability and maintain their integrity using more conventional memory protection mechanisms. Such schemes typically require capabilities to be created and interpreted by software.

Efficiency

A major advantage of capability mechanisms is their efficiency.[23] Presentation and interpretation of a capability is efficient because the capability is easily located when not immediately available. Additionally, it is not necessary to perform name evaluation of the subject on each access attempt, only when the capability is generated. If a capability refers to an object directly, rather than through a naming system, then name evaluation for the target object is also eliminated at access time, providing further efficiency benefits.

Distribution of capabilities

The properties of capabilities that enable efficient evaluation mechanisms pose other inevitable problems. These result primarily from the distribution of capabilities, plus the reduced frequency of name evaluation and name protection binding.

ACL mechanisms achieve rigorous enforcement of authorisation state changes by centralisation of mechanisms and data; capability systems allow the protected data to be distributed. A significant issue concerns rights revocation, when it is required to remove the right of a subject to access an object. The problem is that the capabilities granting the revoked access are not easily or efficiently located. A number of schemes have been devised to address this problem:

1. The use of back-pointers to capabilities.[24]

2. Periodic deletion of capabilities, such that reacquisition is required (at which point it may be denied).[25]

3. Storing capabilities in protected areas, such that they are easily located. Capabilities are then referenced indirectly, so that they are easily located for deletion, at which time all indirect capabilities referring to them are invalidated for subsequent access attempts (*see* Figure 4.14).

Indirection

Indirection is an important technique used when constructing viable capability systems,[26] allowing a central set of capabilities to be maintained in order that issues of control (revocation, authorisation state changes, etc) and protection (the need to store capabilities securely in the absence of specialised architectures) are simplified.

By way of example, Figure 4.15 illustrates a situation where access to object 02 is via the central capability number 2. To allow efficient revocation of access rights to this object, the various subjects requiring access to 02 are each given a different local capability, pointing to the central capability number 2. Revocation is efficiently achieved by deleting capability number 2, thus invalidating all local capabilities that refer to it. Under such a scheme, it may then be necessary to re-issue local capabilities to authorised subjects, and to use back-pointers or garbage collection schemes to clear out invalid capabilities from the system.

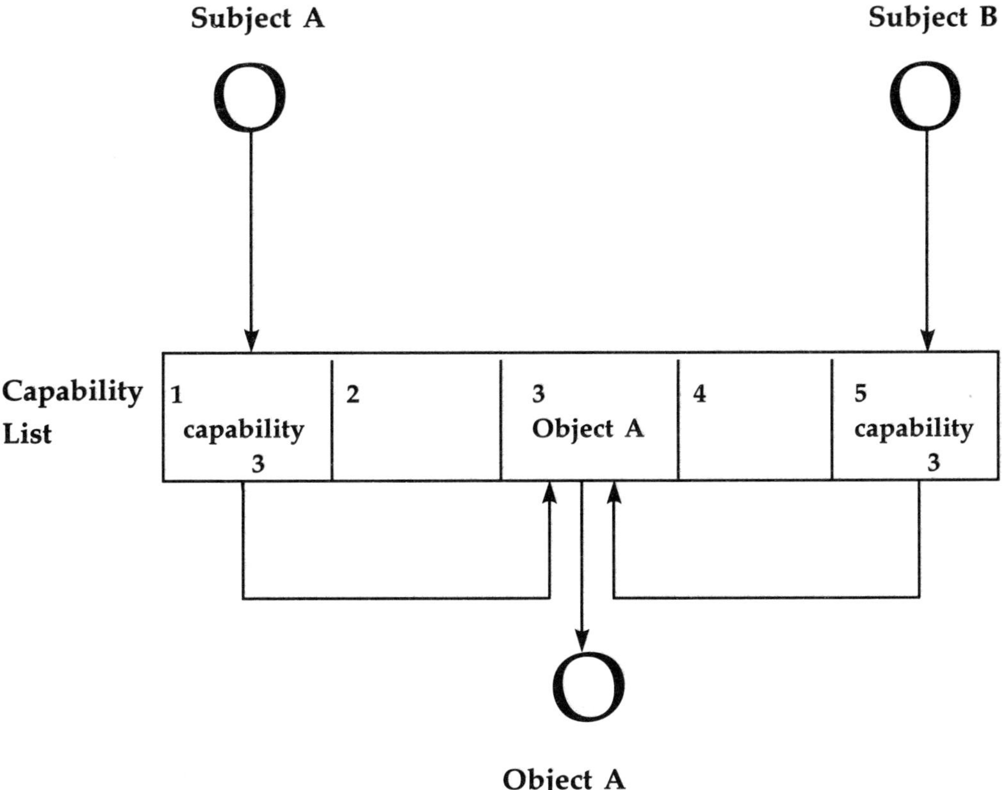

Figure 4.14 Use of Indirection in Capability Systems

Centralised capability lists

The centralised capability list represents the total set of access rights available within the system. Individual protection domains (with the possible exception of one domain representing the maximum possible access rights) require that only subsets of the capability list be available. This requirement equates with the requirement to construct local address spaces from the total set of addresses supported by the system. The fundamental concept is that protection domains are constructed by a mechanism that selects a subset of the central capability set.[27] Local addresses for capabilities may be constructed as terse references into local indirection tables,[28] which in turn are mapped into the central C-list by an appropriate selection function (*see* Figure 4.15).

Other notable advantages of capability based mechanisms are:

- The ability to construct small protection domains, in keeping with the principle of least privilege;

- The provision of both object naming and protection at runtime;

- The binding between high-level names (such as character string filenames) and capabilities (which are generally small objects) may be performed using directories to hold (name, capability) pairs.[29]

If a domain does not contain excessive privilege, then a domain switch to a more privileged domain will require that the rights associated with capabilities be increased. A mechanism for achieving this is known as 'rights amplification'.[30] The scheme works by defining 'amplification templates', which are triples of the form (object identity, old rights, new rights). During a domain switch, a capability in the 'old' domain that matches the identity and rights fields in the amplification template becomes a capability of the form (identity, new rights) in the 'new' domain.[31] This is essentially an application of a lock and key protection mechanism, with the 'old rights' providing the lock/key combination.

Combined ACL and Capability Mechanisms

It is possible to devise protection mechanisms that employ a combination of ACL and capability schemes. Initially, access permission is checked using an ACL, and a capability is issued if access is authorised.

An example is commonly implemented to enable efficient access to disk files. When a process wishes to open a file, the file system will consult an ACL

A capability based memory management scheme using local capability segments, referencing objects indirectly via a central capability segment. Rights revocation in such a scheme may be achieved by invalidating the central capability for an object.

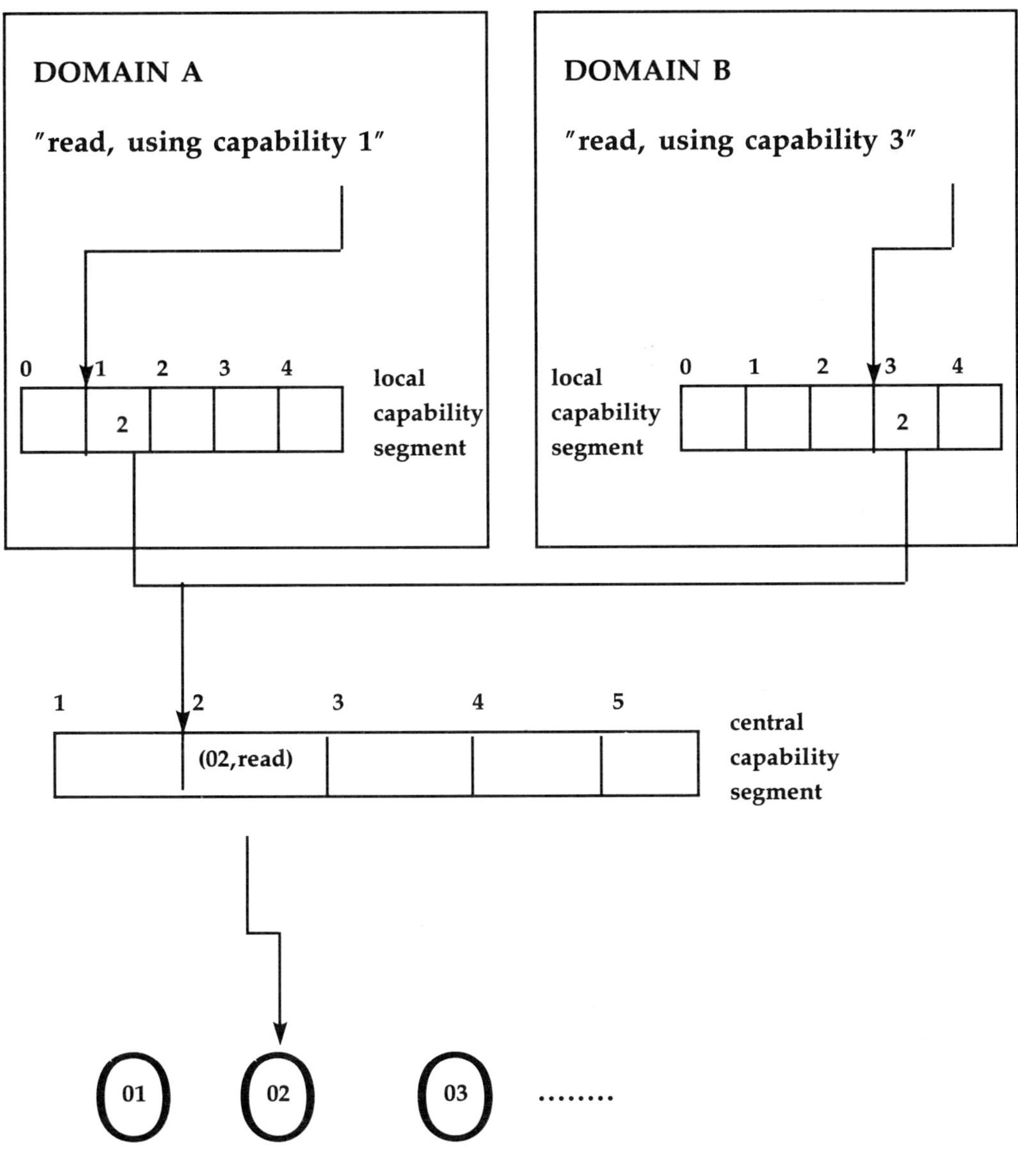

Figure 4.15 Capability Based Memory Management

associated with the file to determine if access should be granted. If the requested access is authorised, the file system will build the data structures needed to support access to the file and return a data item to the process which is presented, when requesting subsequent efficient access to the file. In many cases the data item is forged in a trivial way, in other cases not so. While the use of the data item to select between open files is needed, since the same file may have been opened several times but with different modes, it is nonetheless a type of capability implemented in software.

Access Controls Using Passwords

Passwords are used in some access control mechanisms as a type of capability object, such that access to an object is granted on presentation of the appropriate password. Such schemes are simple to design and implement and are employed in such contemporary systems as VM/SP, MVS/XA and MS-DOS. Access to a password protected resource is granted by releasing the password for the resource to authorised users. This results in passwords being distributed throughout the system, in a variety of containers. As was observed in an early paper on protection:

> "such systems have nothing to recommend them save economy of mechanism." (*Lampson B W, 1969*).

4.6 THE CONFINEMENT PROBLEM

Conventional protection mechanisms allow programs to be constrained in terms of the objects they may access. There are many cases in which unauthorised information transfer may still occur in spite of such controls, using objects or signalling mechanisms not covered by the protection mechanisms. This allows confidentiality aspects of a security policy to be undermined, and is a major concern in highly sensitive systems such as many military systems. It therefore constitutes a major aspect of the TCSEC above class B1. The problem is essentially one of information flow control, and is known as the confinement or 'covert channel' problem.[32] There are two types of covert channel, storage and timing.

Covert Channels

Storage channels use some attribute or property of the system to provide a signalling mechanism, such as filelocks, filenames or buffer pools. In all cases these may be considered as finite resource pools (containing one instance of the resource in the case of unique filelocks and filenames), which may be exhausted and tested for exhaustion as part of a signalling scheme. In essence, the system stores the signal being sent.

Timing (or modulation) channels depend upon being able to influence the rate at which some other process is able to acquire resources such as the use of shared I/O devices, processor cycles and memory (via paging or dynamic allocation). This variation in rate may be used to pass signals. Timing channels are normally considerably less efficient than storage channels, having a reduced bandwidth, but are also typically harder to control.

Storage channels can often be transformed into timing channels by delaying response to a process requesting an exhausted resource type. However, these limitations can be addressed by the use of efficient encoding schemes and other techniques derived from information theory (such as error correction codes). Further, it may be possible to increase transmission rates by constructing parallel covert communications. For example, in the case of the file interlock scheme, if eight files are used then these may be locked in a pattern corresponding to an eight-bit character code, so that the communication channel is now one byte wide.

The TCSEC includes guidelines on covert channels, as these must be identified and controlled in systems above level B1. It suggests that channels with a band-width of less than one bit per second are acceptable for most applications, and that channels with bandwidths in excess of one bit per second should be audited.[33]

The problem of limiting or removing covert channels within the operating system requires analysis of the TCB interface, the storage objects plus information channels implemented by the operating system, and rectifying each of these (perhaps individually). While conceptually straightforward, the effort required to achieve this in an operating system of any complexity may be enormous, and will be exacerbated by the assurances of correctness required if the operating system itself is to be accepted as trusted. This problem cannot usually be solved without significant performance overheads, since it may be necessary to generate spurious resource utilisation, in order to prevent potential leakages. The unattractiveness of such solutions is such that it is normal to accept a compromise on covert channels by restricting their capacity, rather than eliminating them entirely.

In practice, covert channels tend to be easier to control in systems with a mandatory MLS mechanism (those at or above level B1 of the TCSEC). Subsequent discussions concentrate on issues of covert channels, which are by far the more difficult to detect and control.

The identification of covert channels is typically a difficult task, which the shared resources matrix methodology is intended to assist. It can be successfully used at all stages of system development, being equally applicable to natural language statements, formal specifications and programming language implementations.[34]

The methodology recognises that two types of covert channel exist, these being storage channels and timing channels. In both cases the only channels of interest are those that breach the security policy, with channels that parallel legitimate communication paths being of lesser concern.

The conditions that must hold for a storage channel to exist differ from those of a timing channel. However, a common condition for both types of channel is that the transmitting and receiving objects over the channel must have access to a shared resource attribute, which in the case of a file could include such attributes as its name, locks, protection data, contents or I/O buffer. Access to a shared resource attribute does not necessarily imply access rights to the object itself, but for example, the ability to use a pre-selected filename which may only exist uniquely as a signalling mechanism (ie conflicting attempts to create a file of the same name).

The shared resource matrix methodology involves two phases. First, potential covert channels are identified. Secondly, each potential channel is analysed in detail to determine whether a channel actually exists, and if so what its bandwidth is. The shared resource matrix methodology actually addresses only the first of these phases, with the second depending upon such manual inspection or testing techniques as are considered appropriate.

4.7 CRYPTOGRAPHY

Cryptographic systems protect information by means of data transformations. The transformations are called *'encipherment'*, or *'encryption'* when the transformation is from the original 'cleartext' representation to the corresponding 'ciphertext' representation. The transformations are called *'decipherment'* or *'decryption'* when the transformation is from ciphertext to the original cleartext.

A formal description of a cryptographic system is useful and establishes a notation for use in later discussions.[35]

The cryptographic system has the following components:

1. A plaintext message space, M

2. A ciphertext message space, C

3. A key space, K

4. A set of enciphering transformations, E_k M C, where k is a key selected from K

5. A set of deciphering transformations, D_k C M, where k is a key selected from K

The enciphering and deciphering transformations are such that there is a standard enciphering algorithm and a standard deciphering algorithm. The algorithms are dependent upon keys selected from the keyspace K, where each key selects a different transformation from the set of available transformations (for both encipherment and decipherment transformations). For a given key k, the enciphering transformation E_k and the deciphering transformation D_k are inverses, such that $D_k(E_k(m) = m$ for all members of M.

Cryptography Schemes

Cryptographic schemes are used as a protection mechanism in information systems in two principle ways. One is to protect the secrecy of information, such that the unauthorised acquisition of information is prevented. The other is to protect information against unauthorised modification, including creation, alteration or destruction. The properties required of a cryptographic system are different for each of the above and are referred to as 'secrecy' and 'authenticity' considerations.

It is possible to describe general requirements for all cryptographic systems and also the additional requirements needed to achieve secrecy and authenticity in cryptographic systems.[36]

The general requirements for cryptographic systems are:

1. The cryptographic transformations must be efficient for all keys.

2. The system must be easy to use.

3. The security of the system should only depend on the secrecy of the keys, not the algorithm that uses the keys.

Confidentiality requirements of cryptographic systems are, that unless the cipher key in question is known:

1. Given ciphertext, even given the corresponding cleartext, it is computationally unfeasible to systematically deduce the deciphering transformation.

2. Given ciphertext, it is computationally unfeasible to systematically determine the corresponding cleartext.

Confidentiality requirements, therefore, depend only on the integrity of the deciphering transformation, ie enciphered data cannot be recovered without the appropriate key.

Authenticity requirements of cryptographic systems are, that unless the cipher key in question is known:

1. Given ciphertext, even given the corresponding cleatext, it is computationally unfeasible to determine the enciphering transformation.

2. It is computationally unfeasible to determine ciphertext that produces valid plaintext when a specific deciphering transformation is applied to it.

Authenticity requirements depend only upon the integrity of the enciphering transformation.

General Cryptographic Attacks

Two general types of attack are recognised as threatening information systems protected by cryptographic technique:

Passive attacks involve the analysis of intercepted ciphertext in attempts to recover the information encoded therein. Such attacks are difficult to detect since no detrimental effects may be produced on the performance of the information system concerned.

Active attacks attempt to change information in systems protected by cryptographic techniques. Active attacks are countered by cryptographic authenticity techniques, which may be used to detect amendments or insertions to ciphertext.

The attacks on cryptosystems may be further classified according to the amount of information available to the cryptanalyst. In ciphertext-only attacks, the cryptanalyst has only ciphertext available, whereas in a known-plaintext attack a cryptanalyst has samples of ciphertext and the corresponding cleartext. A third classification is the chosen-plaintext attack, in which the cryptanalyst has not merely samples of ciphertext and cleartext pairs, but may choose the examples which will be of most use to the cryptanalytic process. These classifications are given in order of increasing benefit to the cryptanalyst. Strong cryptographic systems are expected to withstand chosen-plaintext attacks without loss of reliability.

The general requirement is largely concerned with the enciphering algorithm. It is dependent on the size of the keyspace (ie the number of keys available) and message space, such that the number of trials required in an exhaustive search is not impractical. Encryption algorithms are of two types:

Symmetric algorithms use the same key in both enciphering and deciphering transformations. Such systems closely relate secrecy and integrity considerations, since knowledge of the enciphering transformation exposes the deciphering transformation and vice versa.

Asymmetric encryption algorithms use different keys for the encipherment and decipherment transformations, and require that at least one of the keys is computationally unfeasible to determine, given the other. In asymmetric systems, one of the transformations may be used for secrecy, the other for integrity.

Asymmetric or 'public key' cryptosystems must possess four properties:[37]

1. Plaintext is recovered if first enciphered then deciphered, ie $D(E(M)) = M$

2. Both the enciphering and deciphering transformations are easy to compute.

3. The deciphering transformation cannot easily be determined given knowledge of the enciphering transformation.

4. Plaintext is recovered if first deciphered then enciphered, ie $E(D(M)) = M$.

Functions that satisfy properties 1 through to 3 are called 'trap-door one-way functions'. Those that satisfy 1 through to 4 are called 'trap-door one-way permutations'. They are 'one-way' in that they are easily computed in one direction, but difficult to compute in the inverse direction. However, given certain additional (secret) 'trap-door' information, the inverse function also becomes easy to compute. Property 4 implies that the mapping between plaintext and ciphertext is a bijection (ie it is 'one to one' and 'onto'), in that a given plaintext message is the enciphered form of some other plain-text message and a given ciphertext message is the deciphered form of some other ciphertext message (this property allows the construction of digital signatures).

The Data Encryption Standard

In 1973 and 1974, the US National Bureau of Standards issued notices soliciting algorithms as candidates for a standard encryption algorithm.[38] IBM submitted an algorithm in 1974, which was considered to be the only acceptable algorithm among those submitted. It was published first as a draft standard in 1975, then as a Federal standard in 1977, from when it has been known as the Data Encryption Standard or simply DES. Since then it has become extremely common throughout the world. The DES was originally expected to have a ten year lifetime, and indeed after almost exactly this period the NBS announced that the DES would no longer be ratified as a standard. A key consideration in this decision was the popularity of the DES, in that the enticement to develop a scheme or mechanism for breaking the DES was becoming unacceptable, so great had the potential rewards become.

Nevertheless, the DES remains a 'de facto' standard in most respects, and despite concerns over its key-space of 2^{56}, has apparently withstood cryptanalytic attacks.

The Data Encryption Standard (DES)[39] defines a block cipher producing 64-bit output blocks as a function of a 64-bit input block and a

56-bit key. The DES is specifically intended for implementation in hard-ware.

Data Encryption Algorithm (DEA)

The DEA is a product cipher, meaning that it combines both substitution and transposition operations. The transposition functions in particular were designed to achieve strong inter-symbol dependency[40] such that each bit of the output block is a complex function of all bits of the input block and all significant bits of the key.[41] The DES takes a 64-bit input value and produces a 64-bit output value dependent on a 56-bit key (supplied as a 64-bit quantity with one redundant bit per byte).[42]

The DES makes extensive use of permutation operations, defined by mapping tables. These map bits of an input quantity onto pseudo-random bits of an output quantity. The DES also makes extensive use of modulo-2 bitwise addition between bit vectors, ie as implemented in the exclusive-OR (XOR) operation found in many contemporary computer architectures. This latter operation has the property that while a first operation disguises the original value, a second identical operation completely restores it, and it is this property that allows the DES to exploit essentially the same algorithm for both encryption and decryption.

When the DES is operated, the input value is permuted immediately on input and again immediately prior to being output. Between these two permutation operations, the high order and low order halves of the value are successively XORed with a series of 32-bit values returned by the 'f' function. The 'f' function takes as its input the other half of the 64-bit value and a 48-bit value derived from the supplied encryption key. This iterative operation is performed 16 times. On each iteration the key derivative is different, generated by bit shifting operations performed on the key derivative value used in the preceding iteration and then permuting the result. The sequence of key derivative values used during encryption is used in reverse order during decryption, otherwise the algorithm performs identically for both encryption and decryption.

The 'f' function itself is also internally quite straightforward. Its input 32-bit value is expanded into a 48-bit value using a selection table (some bits being used twice). The resultant 48-bit value is XORed with the 48-bit key derivative also input to the 'f' function. The result is treated as a sequence of eight 6-bit values, each of which is input to a different 's-box' function. Each of the eight 's-box' functions uses bits selected from its 6-bit input to form indices into a local two-dimensional table and returns the 4-bit value stored therein. The output from the eight 's-boxes' is thus a sequence of 4-bit values forming a 32-bit quantity. This 32-bit quantity is subject to a permutation operation before being returned as the output of the 'f' function.

The DES functions are non-linear and complex, such that it is highly difficult to describe the DES mappings mathematically. This is an intentional design arm of the DES, in order to overcome the difficulty of deterministic attacks based upon analysis of the DES functions.[43] Although hardware implementations of the DES achieve throughput of up to 10Mbps,[44] throughput of a software implementation will typically be much lower due to the inefficiency of the algorithm when implemented in software.

DES Modes of operation

The DEA algorithm may be used in a variety of ways that are not constrained by the size of the DEA input and output blocks. It is possible, using these techniques to produce cipher systems that hide the statistical nature of data recurring in many 64-bit blocks, or to produce stream cipher systems operating perhaps on single bits of multiples thereof (up to a maximum of 64). The standard techniques, or 'modes of operation' are described in a standards publication.[45]

Electronic Code Book

The Electronic Code Book (ECB) uses the DEA as a block cipher, with each input and output block being the full 64 bit size. Input is handled in units of 64-bit blocks and since any two identical input blocks encipher to identical ciphertext, characteristics of input text may be exposed in the ciphertext. Further, ECB mode does not offer strong integrity properties, in that an individual cipher block within a message (for example an encrypted timestamp) could be altered or replaced (by the corresponding block from another message) which ECB encryption alone would not detect.

Cipher Block Chaining

The Cipher Block Chaining (CBC) technique also uses the DEA as a block cipher. It differs from the ECB mode, in that blocks are 'chained' such that a dependency exists between a given block and the immediately preceding block (an 'initialisation vector' being used in the case of the first block), such that each block is actually dependent upon all the preceding blocks.

The 'chaining' effect is achieved prior to encryption by performing bitwise modulo-2 addition (exclusive OR) between an input block and the encrypted form of the previous block and inputting the result to the DEA to produce the next enciphered block. In the case of the first block a 64-bit 'initialisation vector' (IV) is used, which should be chosen as a pseudo-random value and suitably protected.

Decipherment under CBC mode first transforms a ciphertext block using the DEA in decipherment mode. This 'deciphered' block is restored to plaintext by performing bitwise modulo-2 addition with the fully enciphered form of the previous block (the initialisation vector in the case of the first block).

The dependency between blocks that is introduced in CBC mode results in an error extension characteristic.[46] The final block produced in CBC mode is dependent upon the entire preceding message in a similar fashion to error-detection codes, but has the additional cryptographic properties of functional dependency on the cryptographic key. Further, the inter-bit dependency of the DEA is such that leading bits from the final CBC block may be used (as opposed to the entire block) as a Message Authentication Code (MAC). The MAC technique offers an integrity check mechanism for data (which may also be enciphered for secrecy) in that a MAC attached to data cannot be computed without knowing the correct key, hence the data cannot be falsified.

On receipt of a message, the MAC can be recalculated, and will detect any alteration to the message with a probability of $1-(2^{-n})$, where n is the length of the MAC (between 1 and 64 bits). The CBC mode will produce the same ciphertext and thus the same MAC for two identical input messages. Additional safeguards are necessary to prevent the deletion of entire messages, reordering of the message stream or replay of (recordings of) previous messages. It is recommended that a unique Message Identifier be incorporated in each message, which may be inspected upon receipt in order to detect these types of attack.

In CBC mode, corruption of n bits in an enciphered block effects the decipherment of that block and its successor. The decipherment of the corrupt block will result in each output bit being incorrect with a probability of 0.5, due to the DEA property that each output bit is functionally dependent on every bit of the input (and every bit of the key). The output of the next DEA operation, assuming there is no corruption to its input will have the n corruptions introduced into it by the CBC decipherment exclusive OR operation. Subsequent blocks remain unaffected.

It is necessary for the 64-bit block boundaries to remain synchronised between encipherment and decipherment operations in CBC mode. CBC does have a self-synchronisation property however, whereby the effect of lost synchronisation disappears within 64-bits of synchronisation being recovered. Although originally intended for protecting the integrity of messages transmitted over an insecure communications link, when equivalent authenticity requirements arise within a computing system, techniques based on MACs may appropriately be employed. Thus, for example, a highly trusted subsystem may safely use the storage facilities of a less trusted subsystem by protecting stored data with MACs. Thus MAC techniques may be considered whenever a relationship exists between three communicating entities such that A communicates with C via B, yet A and C desire proof that B has not altered the messages between them. Note that B may be a passive storage device accessible to other entities. A and C may be the same entity (A = C).

Cipher Feedback Mode

The Cipher Feedback mode (CFB) is a stream cipher with properties of error extension (under encipherment) and self-synchronisation.

The DEA is used to produce a stream of n-bit blocks that are used to encrypt a stream of n-bit cleartext blocks by performing exclusive OR between the two blocks. Decryption consists of regenerating the enciphering bit-stream and performing exclusive OR with the encrypted stream.

The blocksize in CFB can be between 1 and 64-bits in size. The CFB mechanism shifts input n-bit quantities into the least significant n bits of the DEA input block, and uses the most significant bits of the DEA output block as an n-bit block of the cipher stream. To initialise the system, an n-bit initialisation vector is used, being shifted into an otherwise zero DEA input block. Subsequent operations use the n-bit cipher-text block from the previous operation (the previous n-bit cipher stream block exclusive OR'd with the previous n-bit cleartext block) as the value to be shifted into the DEA input block. This results in a dependency between cipher stream blocks and the preceding cipher text blocks, in a similar fashion to that of CBC. Thus, the CFB mode has the property of self-synchronisation for n-bit blocks, and can be used for message authentication.

In CFB mode, the production of the cipher stream is performed using the DEA in enciphering mode. As with CBC, the value of the initialisation vector should be carefully chosen and protected. The recommendations for CFB recognise that many commercial DES implementations work efficiently on 8-bit inputs, while many digital systems use 7-bit character codes. A standard recommendation, referred to as the 7-bit CFB mode, allows efficient use of DES in such cases by always setting the high-order bit (typically parity) of a byte to 1, and using the low-order bits to pass a 7-bit character code. A further variation on this allows this technique of padding 7-bit characters into 8-bit DES inputs to be applied across more than one of the DES input byte boundaries. It is considered acceptable (for US government applications) to use the DES with up to eight fixed input bits, as would be the case if this technique were applied to all eight possible DES input bytes.

Output Feedback Mode

The Output Feedback (OFB) mode uses the DEA as an additive stream cipher. The DEA is used to produce a cipher stream on n-bit blocks (where n is less than 64), with encryption and decryption being performed by adding an n-bit cipher-stream block to an n-bit block from a data stream (cleartext or ciphertext) in a bitwise modulo-2 operation (exclusive OR).

The OFB mode is initiated by shifting an n-bit initialisation vector into the low order n-bits of the DEA input, and operating the DEA in enciphering mode. The most significant n bits from the DEA output are used to encipher/decipher an n-bit block from a data stream, and are also shifted into the low order n bits of the DEA input block for the next iteration of the process. The OFB mode cannot be used to produce MACs since no ciphertext chaining is performed. Neither is the OFB a self synchronising cipher mechanism, so that the cipher system (enciphering and deciphering operations) must be completely resynchronised in the event that the n-bit boundary synchronisation is lost.

The RSA Algorithm

The Rivest, Shamir, Adleman (RSA) public key encryption scheme, first published in 1978, is the predominant example of an asymmetric encryption scheme.[47] Under the RSA scheme, messages are represented by integers in the interval 0 to (n-1), for a chosen value of n. The mapping between meaningful messages and integers is unimportant and may be simply achieved by dividing messages into a series of byte multiples of the appropriate length.

The enciphering and deciphering transformations are made by raising the input integer to different integer powers (for encryption and decryption) modulo n. Thus for plaintext M and ciphertext C, $C = E(M) = M^e \bmod n$, $M = E(M) = C^d \bmod n$. The public key is the integer pair (e,n), and the secret key is the integer pair (d,n). The RSA algorithm implements a trapdoor one-way permutation, thus may be used to construct digital signatures.

The strength of the RSA algorithm depends largely on the difficulty of factoring large numbers. The value of n is computed as the product of two large primes, p and q, each of the order of 100 decimal digits in size. The value of n is thus of the order of 200 digits, which would take approximately 3.8×10^9 years to factorise, using the fastest algorithm known to the originators of the RSA at one operation per microsecond.

While the value of n is made public, the values of p and q are kept secret and, in fact, may be discarded once the values of the public and private key pairs have been chosen.

In addition to being large primes, it is recommended that p and q satisfy a number of additional properties in order to prevent successful factorisation attempts of n using sophisticated algorithms. The recommendations are:

1. The values of p and q should differ by a few digits in length.

2. Both (p-1) and (q-1) should contain large prime factors.

3. The greatest common divisor of (p-1) and (q-1) should be small.

The second element, d, of the secret key pair is chosen as an integer greater than p or q, and which is relatively prime to ((p-1)(q-1).

The second element, e, of the public key pair is computed as the multiplicative inverse of d modulo (p-1)(q-1), that is $ed \bmod 0(n) = 1$.

Given that e and d satisfy the identity $ed \bmod 0\ (n) = 1$ the enciphering and deciphering transformations are mutual inverses, ie $(M^e \bmod n)^d \bmod n = M$.

The authors of the RSA algorithm suggest efficient algorithms for performing exponentiation of integers modulo n, for discovering large primes and for computing inverses (ie for obtaining e).

4.8 CRYPTOGRAPHIC APPLICATIONS IN COMMUNICATION SYSTEMS

The predominant use of cryptographic systems is in telecommunication systems, where cryptographic techniques often present the only viable protection mechanism and are becoming increasingly important in operating systems, due to the increase in networked and distributed operating systems.

The issues that must be addressed in secure communication systems are:[48]

1. To prevent disclosure of plaintext in the absence of the deciphering key. This is an instance of a fundamental secrecy requirement of cryptographic systems.

2. To prevent unauthorised release of information by the sender. The requirement here is to prevent the unauthorised transfer of information by untrustworthy components within an end system, including scenarios where the illicit transfer protocol is not detectable by the authorised recipient (such as when addressed to other end-points or by deliberately causing breach of communication protocols using a signalling mechanism).

3. To permit detection of modifications to messages, including insertion, deletion, modification or transposition of message contents. This is an instance of a fundamental authenticity requirement of cryptographic systems.

4. To permit assurances that sequences of messages are complete and in the correct sequence. This requires the ability to detect message insertion, deletion or rearrangement, including those at the beginning or end of a sequence.

5. To permit the verification of a message's origin and destination, such that message end-points cannot be falsified and redirection of messages is prevented.

6. To permit the timeliness of messages to be verified, in particular to enable detection of 'replays' of previous valid message sequences.

7. To permit detection of falsified acknowledgements of message receipt.

8. To combine the above such that any change of message content, sequence, timeliness or acknowledgement may be detected.

9. To offer the above, protective measures to cater for end-to-end protection between end-points in systems involving (groups or classes of) many end-points, including packet switched networks and broadcast transmission techniques.

10. To prevent fraudulent disavowal of messages and the falsification of signed messages. The techniques applied in this area are usually referred to as digital signatures, and the property of preventing fraudulent disavowal is usually referred to as the property of 'non-repudiation'.

11. To prevent unauthorised acquisition of information by 'traffic analysis', that is, to prevent knowledge imparted by determining the amount (or other statistical properties) of traffic, flowing between pairs or sets of communicating end-points.

Integrity requirements usually demand that issues 3,4,5,6 and 7 of those lists be satisfied and may also demand that issues 8,9 and 10 be satisfied. Confidentiality requirements usually demand that issues 1 and 2 be satisfied, and may in addition require that issue 11 be satisfied.

Communication protocols are fundamental in solving several of the these issues. Communication protocols that make provisions for checksums, sequence numbering, source identification, destination identification and timestamping address aspects of issues 3 through to 5 inclusively. In the absence of cryptographic protection however, the communication protocol is easily subverted by modification of transmission frame fields. Hence, it is usual to achieve communication system security through a combination of cryptographic and protocol techniques.

4.9 CRYPTOGRAPHIC SEALING

As an example of a cryptographic technique useful in distributed operating systems, we will consider the passive technique of cryptographic sealing, which can be used to implement protection mechanisms within a computer system.[49] Objects are protected by encrypting or 'sealing' them, using combinations of symmetric and asymmetric cryptographic schemes. The sealed object includes a checksum, calculated from the value of the decrypted object, that allows the decrypt primitive to verify that decryption has taken place, ie that the correct key has been used in the decryption operation.

Note that this assurance is not absolute, and that correct decryption will sometimes be assumed when it has not been achieved, therefore the probability of this happening is based on the strength of the algorithm and size of the checksum used.

Additionally, sealed objects may be nested such that the encrypted object may contain one or more encryption key objects which may be recovered and used as part of the 'unseal' primitive allowing implementation of protection schemes based upon multiple encryption.

The protection schemes that may be implemented using cryptographic sealing depend upon relationships between the keys used to seal and unseal objects. Functions are defined for producing keys that may be used in sealing operations, where an 'unseals' relationship is defined between a set of keys and an individual key.

The unseal primitive attempts to unseal an object using one or more of the keys available to a requesting process, such that possession of keys determines which objects may be unsealed. The recursive nature of unseals means that keys recovered from an object, as a result of initial attempts to unseal the object, may be used in further unseal operations until the original sealed item is recovered or the operation fails.

The ability to construct flexible protection mechanisms using the concepts of sealing is improved by techniques allowing more sophisticated relationships to be defined between sealed keys and the keys (or sets thereof) that unseal them. The ability to recover cleartext from sealed objects is dependent on the set of keys initially supplied to the unseal primitive, since this set of keys must be sufficient to unseal either the object itself or one or more key objects contained therein. The concept of a security domain is thus related to this set of keys.

The suggested means of protecting this set of keys for a given principle (referred to as a 'key ring') is to seal it under a key supplied as part of the sign-on sequence. Capability schemes may be implemented using sealing in a straightforward fashion.

The ability to read an object depends upon possession of a key unsealing it. The ability to write to an object must depend, however, upon some additional mechanism. A suggested approach is to use a simple active mechanism requiring that a secret ('guard') value, which is sealed within the object, be provided when requesting write access.

Access control lists may also be implemented using a cryptographic sealing scheme. This may be achieved using asymmetric encryption to construct a public key scheme. ACL entries, containing keys (and guards) for unsealing the associated object, are sealed under a key-or scheme using the public keys of all users authorised to access the object (each user being responsible for generating and publicising their public keys). The ACL entries may be unsealed by those users with their secret key, when the key sealing the associated object is obtained.

4.10 ERROR CONTROL CODES

Error control codes exist that may be used for detection and correction of errors in associated fields of information. Here we are only interested in error detection, which is simpler than error correction.

When used in computing systems, such codes are commonly referred to as Cyclic Redundancy Codes, and strong codes can detect errors with a probability of $1-(2^{-n})$, where n is the size of the checksum in bits.[50]

Conventional error detection codes can be constructed to provide a high assurance that random errors in data will be detected, but it is not difficult to circumvent them as an authentication code. Thus, it is possible to introduce chosen changes into a message, such that the new message also produces the original checksum. This arises due to the simplicity of the checksum algorithm and the fact that this algorithm is public. For example, this can be achieved for long messages where all of the message except the last n bits, where n is the length of the CRC code, are freely chosen. The last n bits are then chosen to generate the required code.

Although conventional error correction codes do not offer a strong authentication technique, a related technique known as 'finger-printing' does. This technique is similar to encryption in that it allows the selection of a secret 'generator polynomial', used in the calculation of an error detection code, out of a large set of generator polynomials.

4.11 AUTHENTICATION

Authentication is an activity that verifies identity between either or both of the entities involved in an authentication dialogue. There are two types of authentication that are normally of interest. The first is authentication of users signing on to a system. The second is authentication of computers that are cooperating in a networked or distributed environment.

First, we consider the issue of authenticating system users and secondly, we include an example of how peer-authentication can be achieved between two computing systems. This is an increasingly important aspect of the security of networked and distributed operating systems.

User Authentication

Generally, user authentication relies upon information about the person being transferred to the authentication agent. The information may relate to one or more of:

- Something known by the person, such as a password or PIN value.

- Something possessed by the person, such as a magnetic stripe card.

- Some morphological or physiological attribute of the person, such as delivered by handwritten signature scanners or retina scanners.

It has been observed that absolute identity verification cannot be achieved, although the interaction performing user authentication may be arbitrarily complicated. This characteristic arises because, for example, passwords may be guessed, tokens lost and physiological attributes liable to misinterpretation. It is also a characteristic of certain user authentication techniques, that a risk of compromise is associated with their use, for example, a significant risk of disclosing a password or PIN occurs at the time and place of its entry. In the case of passwords specifically, techniques for controlling password selection and password lifetime are among those used to manage the inherent risks of these systems.

A Review of Password Techniques

Passwords provide a simple and convenient mechanism of verifying a claimed user identity. Their abundance is such that they are likely to remain in predominant use for the foreseeable future. A frequent use of passwords within operating systems is as part of protection mechanisms controlling access to resources such as files or computing services, where presentation of the appropriate password is accepted as confirmation that the requested access to the object in question is authorised. This type of mechanism is in principle an instance of a capability based protection mechanism. Although these are described in the chapter on protection mechanisms, some of the considerations given will also apply due to the nature of passwords as a generic type of object.

Furthermore passwords are still commonly used for such purposes as peer-authentication of computing services and as an authorisation mechanism where identity is not established. Both techniques are extremely weak mechanisms, and do not compare favourably with the available alternatives.

User Identification Verification Checks

By far the most familiar and widespread use of passwords is as a user identity verification check involving presentation of a password supposedly known only to the bona fide individual concerned. This type of usage is the context for most of the discussions concerning passwords that appear in the available literature.

A review of this literature shows that opinions vary significantly among commentators as to the best techniques for addressing the various issues that arise in password based system, such as whether to generate passwords in the user access control system[51]or whether to allow users to choose them.[52]

Criteria for Comparison of Password Systems

Comparison of password systems may be based on four characteristics:

- password selection technique;

- password lifetime;

- password characteristics;

- password information content.

A primary requirement for a successful password system is that it is accepted and respected by the user population, since carelessness with passwords may easily result in their compromise and consequent degradation of overall security. A number of somewhat unconventional password schemes have been devised to alleviate some of the risks incurred by conventional password schemes, and are considered next.

Password Selection Techniques

Generally, password values may be chosen by the system user or generated by the password mechanism. In either case, it is essential that the value be easily recalled by the user, but not easily guessed or determined by a would-be impersonator.[53]

User selection of passwords tends to aid memorability, at the expense of predictability. System selected passwords are far more random in content, but tend to be more difficult for users to remember.

The dilemma of user selection as opposed to system selection is typical of that faced in many computer security issues - that of ease of use versus security. The dilemma is particularly poignant in this case due to the reliance of many password systems on human dependability.

Most commentators agree that users naturally tend to choose passwords that are relatively easy to derive and thus not particularly secure. For example, a study of passwords on one system indicated that 86 percent of passwords were easily derived, with one third of the 2831 total disclosed by a five minute, dictionary type programmed search.[54]

In order to reduce the risks inherent in user selection of passwords, it is common to advise user populations as to suitable password lengths and content.[55] Many mechanisms prevent users selecting passwords of below a given length, or selecting previous passwords (by retaining a number of these for comparison). Often however, there are no enforcement mechanisms preventing users from choosing trivial sequences of characters or character strings easily associated with that individual by simple researching (such as car licence plate numbers, telephone numbers and relatives names).

Finally, user selection of passwords avoids problems related to the distribution of system generated passwords (either displayed at the user terminal or assigned by a system administrator) and simplifies the software required to implement the system. An interesting variation of user selected passwords are 'reconstructed' passwords.[56] A reconstructed password may be, for example, a piece of music 'played' on the keyboard, or a sequence of mnemonics from a knitting pattern.

System generated passwords are intended to increase the security of password systems by generating password values with random component properties. This offers a significant improvement on values based on natural language or other highly predictable character combinations. The major problem with such mechanisms tends to be the difficulty people have in remembering long random character strings so that users may have to resort to writing down the password to prevent forgetting it. In such cases the risk of compromise can become high, with user satisfaction and respect for the system diminishing.

In an attempt to improve the recall factor of system generated passwords, the designers of the Multics operating system employed a password generator that produces random combinations of pronounceable characters. Another possibility is the use of passwords assigned by a system administrator. Such systems have the additional risk that each password is known by more than one individual and significant problems of password distribution are encountered.

The psychology of password selection and recall have been studied.[57] The principal results are summarised below:

Berman quotes research results into recall ability for random character strings, stating that people can recall a five character random password with a 98 percent success rate.[58]

Barton considers the properties of password recall based on cognitive processes. Barton's recommended approach is for user selection of passwords based on episodic memory, semantic memory or environmental queueing, combined with distancing the password from the original concept by some readily available process. Thus, to quote one example, episodic memory of Paris is distanced by its association with a line of verse — 'I love Paris in the Springtime', from which the initial characters are used to derive the password ILPITST. Barton states preference for user selection on the basis of improved user acceptance, with acceptable security provided that suitable advice is offered to users, (for example as part of a password change dialogue.) An important element in Barton's scheme is that the prompting concept has highly personal significance to the user, either directly or by association. For example:

(a) Episodic — a distant childhood memory;

(b) Semantic — a randomly chosen concept from common knowedge;

(c) Environmental — a detail from a picture visible from the user's place of work.

Such prompts make the password easier to recall, but only for the individual in question. Distancing of the type exemplified above has the added advantage of removing many of the predictable characteristics of user selected passwords.

Password Lifetime

The lifetime of a password is the time between changes of the password value.

As with encryption keys, frequent changes in value augment security strength by limiting the time available for an exhaustive trial of password values and by limiting the period of exposure following compromise of a password. Due to the limited range of password values (compared to encryption keys) and the potential difficulty in detecting their compromise, such concerns are particularly valid with respect to password systems.[59]

It is usual to recommend that password values be frequently changed.[60] Recognising that system users will often not reliably adhere to such advice, it is also commonplace for password systems to enforce change, typically on the basis of usage counts or elapsed time. The desirable frequency of change is often calculated or illustrated using the concept of safe-time, which is covered below under password characteristics. Password lifetime and usage counts alone, do not address all relevant considerations with respect to a decision on password lifetime. Other critical factors are the frequency of use, transmission and storage risks, risks at entry point (for example, observation of keyboard strokes) and the relevant privilege associated with the password. Many of these factors vary between different user passwords and the different circumstances involving use of the same password (for example, from a secure local location, as opposed to over a public switched connection).

Password Characteristics

Password characteristics are concerned with properties of the password value.

Password space, is defined as the maximum number of allowable password values.[61] For example, in a scheme allowing all six character fields of upper case alphabetic characters, the password space is 26^6.

The concept of password space is relevant to estimation of the risk of exposure through exhaustive (key search) trials. However, if the selection of password values from the password space domain is not random, such as in the case of selections based on natural language (or similarly, phonetic properties), then the size of the key space is deceptive.[62] In such cases, the value will exhibit a predictability, between characters or groups thereof (n-grams) which can be quantified using classical information theory and thus used to direct a systematic search of the key space.[63] Further, unlike a random key space, the number of natural language words does not increase significantly with length.[64] These considerations are among the most cogent for use of system selection of passwords.

Password space may easily be extended by enlarging the character set in use, for example to include digits, upper and lower case, graphic or even non-visible keyboard characters (for example, Escape or Control keys). The resultant effect on the predictability of non-random sequences will depend on the conventions adopted for their use, but may also have adverse effects on user recallability.[65] Similarly, increasing the number of characters constituting a password will increase the password space, and many systems now enforce a minimum length of acceptable password value. Safe-time is a measure of the time required for an effective key search on the password space. Formulae for calculating safe-time have been published.[66] Such formulae are based on the number of password values that must be tried in an exhaustive search, the probability that a given attempt succeeds and the time taken for each attempt (which is subject to local circumstances).

A common recommendation for increasing safe times is to limit the number of permitted attempts to supply a valid password, followed by temporary terminal suspension (or user name suspension or terminal lockout).

It should be noted that safe-time does not allow for attacks directed at terminal, telecommunications or host computer systems. Neither is any allowance made for accidental and unrecognised disclosure of the password by the system user. In this sense the term 'safe-time' may be somewhat misleading.

Password Information Content

Password may contain some type of information other than or in addition to an authentication parameter field.[67]

One example was at the University of Western Ontario where an information retrieval system used a supplied password as a type of capability object. In this example, a previous password is used to authenticate the user during sign-on.

Alternatively it is possible to incorporate a primitive error detection code within the supplied password. One possible use of this is to allow keying errors to be differentiated from deliberate key search attacks. It is not clear that a key search may not be assisted by such a mechanism, since a simplistic error correction code (as opposed to a cryptographic message authentication code) could easily be calculated for each attempted password to give the impression of innocuous miskeying.

Password Protection

The greatest risk of password compromise is typically due to a lack of conscientiousness on the part of the system user. Passwords may be written on terminals, stored in programmable function key buffers, forgotten or exchanged. The primary solution to such compromises is user education, although much can be done to encourage good practice and to limit risks from within the password mechanism (such as controlled password lifetime).

Passwords stored within a computer system may obviously be protected by the protection mechanisms of the architecture and operating system. It is commonly recognised however, that stored passwords are at risk of exposure either accidentally or through circumvention of host protection mechanisms by skilled staff.[68] The standard solution is to store and compare password values transformed by one-way functions (ie one-way encrypted), and a variety of functions for performing this transformation have been described.[69] For example, a password of less than eight characters may be conveniently encrypted by the DEA algorithm, using a constant as input and the password as the enciphering key.

Many mechanisms involve transmitting a password through a telecommunications network during terminal sign-on, at which point the password is vulnerable to disclosure by passive line tapping. Use of end-to-end link encryption provides protection against such threats, as does the use of encryption facilities in intelligent terminals.[70]

When passwords are assigned by an administrator, or in the case of initial password assignment in a user selection scheme, it is necessary to provide secure transfer of the password between the assigner and the recipient. A number of methods have been described, such as use of trusted messengers or issuing passwords in two parts (with receipt of the first part required before issuing the second part).[71] A useful concept for initial password distribution is that of the expired password,[72] which allows a single use of the supplied password, providing the opportunity for the password to be immediately changed.

One Time Passwords

A one time password is a password that is only valid once.[73] Advantages of such systems are:

- disclosure of the password via telecommunications need not disclose any information concerning subsequent password values (assuming a random sequence of values);

- disclosure of a value has a limited effect, in that it allows for example, one sign-on and the disclosure is more likely to be detected when the authorised individual fails to sign-on as anticipated.

Two basic approaches to one time passwords have been described.[74] The alternative approaches are largely concerned with the issue of distributing the one time password.

First, the password mechanism may advise the user of the next password whenever the user successfully logs in. Alternatively, the user may be supplied with a list of passwords to be used in sequence (a variation on this, to allow synchronisation, would be for the system to prompt with one password, the expected reply being the next password in the sequence).

A third alternative, although a degeneration of the general approach, is the assignment of a one time password for a specific host name space. Where individual identification is not also established, issues of auditing and safe password distribution arise. It should be noted that the random, transient nature of one-time passwords means that it is unlikely that users could successfully recall them from memory. Inevitably then, some more permanent form of recording (for example, a written copy) may exist, and this in turn introduces a risk of unauthorised disclosure.

Virtual Passwords

Virtual passwords use a table of personal information associated with each user, a table of constants, a generation number and a set of algorithms to generate a password value.[75] The password is produced by the algorithms (say one per character in the password) operating on the stored personal data and the generation number. Since the password may be regenerated from the stored information, the password itself need not be stored.

An advantage claimed for this scheme is that it allows passwords of other generations to be recovered or recognised. Thus, if a password were to be disclosed, any attempt to use the old generation password, following the next increment, may be indicative of an impersonation attempt using a compromised password, and appropriate measures would be taken. A similar characteristic may be provided in conventional password systems by comparing an invalid password against a stored list of previous password values.

Handshaking Schemes

In the context of password systems, the term handshaking usually refers to schemes where the user must correctly answer a series of questions, based on personal data available to the password mechanism.[76]

This approach has the benefit that the user is always likely to know the correct answers, but, on the other hand, the answers are not usually secret and are easily researched by a would-be impersonator (in concept, the password space is extremely small). Furthermore, the secure storage and maintenance of such quantities of information presents practical difficulties, indeed the storage of personal information may be subject to legislation.

Duress Passwords

Duress passwords are special passwords intended to allow the system user to signify that they are being pressured to effect entry to the system.[77] The mechanism may then continue as if normal entry had been gained (so as not to expose the individual to further risk), while alerting others to the plight of that individual.

Pass Phrases

Pass phrases are intended to address the problems of low key space in user selected password schemes.[78] Rather than restrict the user to specification of a few characters, typically less than ten, a pass phrase allows the user to specify a whole phrase, say up to 80 characters. It is intended that the phrase would be recallable, but equally not obvious.

A pass phrase may be reduced to a Message Authentication Code using say, cipher block chaining under a standard key. The suggested implementation is DES encryption,[79] using cipher block chain mode[80] to produce a 64-bit MAC. While it is possible for different phrases to produce the same encrypted value, the size of the achieved 64-bit key space (due to the entropy of an 80 character phrase) makes this extremely improbable. For example, consider a password selected from a randomly distributed alphanumeric 64-bit key space, as opposed to a pass phrase achieving an equivalent entropy:[81]

1. 39W14EPOX2MBR

2. Three shoes is not quite enough for five feet, even though iambic.

It has been suggested that the pass phrase is much easier to remember than a randomly distributed password value. Conversely it has been suggested that pass phrases are user-hostile in that they require excessive key strokes, particularly for occasional or novice users.[82]

User Interface Considerations

The user interface to a password system, which is usually some type of visual display unit or Teletype device, has several repercussions.

First, it is prudent to echo-suppress or overstrike the area on the screen into which the user enters the password. This step prevents onlookers from reading the typed password, and should also prevent subsequent recovery of the typed password by operations accessing a screen image buffer held in the memory of a computer or communication device. User friendly interfaces in the nature of help screens or explicit error messages may serve to assist the unfamiliar and unauthorised penetrator,[83] and may therefore be considered dangerous.

Key strike patterns, both visible and audible may allow the relative positions (in respect, say, of the keyboard 'home' keys) of the password characters to be guessed. Careful choice of characters or disabling of audible key strike may be desirable.[84]

The password change dialogue is a suitable point at which to offer the user guidance as to methodologies and risks involved in user password selection.[85]

Multiple, Disjoint Password Spaces

A consideration with major repercussions is the existence of multiple, uncomplementary password mechanisms.

Most operating systems, transaction processing systems, information retrieval and query systems incorporate some form of (often crude) password mechanism. A user requiring access to more than one of these may collect a multitude of passwords. In such situations the user may be forced to keep written lists of passwords, or attempt to maintain all of the systems in parallel with the same password; thus introducing a severe disincentive to change passwords and perhaps exposing other systems to the vulnerabilities of the weakest system. Further, the already difficult task of effectively managing password systems is rapidly compounded, since tasks such as effective auditing become more difficult.

Pass Algorithms

Pass algorithms require the user to authenticate identity by knowledge of some secret algorithm.[86] For example, the system may prompt the user with the generated pseudo-random characters 'BEL', which the user transforms by selecting the next alphabetic character for each character of the prompt, returning the result 'CFM'.

This approach raises a number of concerns:

1. The transformations are likely to be extremely simple in cryptographic terms. It is therefore unlikely that such algorithms could withstand determined cryptanalytic attack and the nature of the mechanism may be regarded by some as an intellectual challenge stimulating penetration attempts.

2. The transformations may be key independent, such that open design is impossible.

3. The quantity of secret authentication data requiring preservation in host services is much greater than with passwords and may have to be retained in cleartext (in the form of object code, source code or both).

4. It is not clear how naive or occasional users can be expected to change their algorithm without relevant programming skills or assistance.

Note that a public library of pass-algorithms from which users select an algorithm, limits the algorithms frequently used and may require publication of the secret algorithms.

Smart Cards

The so-called 'smart card' has received considerable attention recently as an end-authentication mechanism, among a number of other successful applications for these devices. They provide an opportunity for local end-authentication on the basis of both something possessed (the card) and something known (typically a Personal Identification Number or PIN). The card is essentially a combined microprocessor and memory unit implemented in a single silicon chip, which is mounted on a plastic card with the physical dimensions of a magnetic stripe card. The construction of the card prevents its alteration or interrogation by magnetic or other means.

The microprocessor is responsible for executing programs loaded into a reserved area of memory and for protecting other memory areas against unauthorised access. The memory itself is typically between one and eight kilobytes and may be partitioned into several areas, for example:

- An area for internal use only, for example, to contain the owners PIN, which usually cannot be altered once stored.

- A program area containing the microprocessor program code. Typically this can only be written into or interrogated during construction of the card, after which memory control contacts are burnt out to prevent access other than instruction fetches by the microprocessor.

- One or more areas reserved for specific applications, allowing a single card to be used for several purposes.

- A dynamic, freely available area for containing work space and public domain information such as the card holder's name.

- An audit trail area used to record details of the card's activity, such as invalid PIN comparisons.

The microprocessor may be used to protect the integrity of the card itself. Typically this would include monitoring a resin based tamper-resistant shield covering the chip, and monitoring for attempts to guess the correct PIN value. In the event of detecting attempted abuse, the microprocessor may erase the memory contents, thereby preventing exposure of its contents and invalidating the card for further use.

Smart cards are used in conjunction with a device for reading and interacting with the card, this device is itself normally constructed to be tamper-resistant. The first interaction with such a device would normally be an authentication dialogue, without which the card would not participate in any other type of interaction. The objective of this authentication is to authenticate the card holder to the card, normally by entering a PIN at a keypad built into the card reader although biometric devices are of increasing interest.

Smart card applications have included home banking, medical record storage and student records. In this context their primary importance is simply that of an end-authentication mechanism. Much of the standard microprocessor code provides powerful authentication functions, including encryption routines, PIN comparison, message authentication and the generation of responses to authentication challenges. These functions mean that smart cards may be used as a secure repository for encryption keys, passwords or protection data such as capability type objects. Further, because they are programmable they can protect information using cryptographic techniques before releasing it into any untrusted communication medium. This enables local authentication to be performed before entering into a secure authentication dialogue with a remote system, such as a large Mainframe, at which stage digital signature techniques may be employed using the functions provided by the card.

The function of smart cards may be expected to increase in the future, as more powerful microprocessors and larger memories become available. For example, a chip implementing the DES algorithm, albeit of limited throughput, is reputed to be under development at the time of writing.

Personal Cryptographic Authenticators

Personal authentication devices of similar physical dimensions to electronic pocket calculators are commercially available, and perform authentication based on something possessed (ie the device) and something known (a Personal Identification Number or PIN). They are used in place of conventional passwords, with the user entering a value generated by the device instead of a password. Each of these devices are typically primed with a key associated with a given user and known also to the host computer performing authentication. Further, the correct PIN must be entered into the device each time it is used.

The device generates a value that is functionally dependent on:

- The key stored within the device;

- The PIN entered by the user;

- Either the time or a pseudo-random number broadcast by the host and entered into the device by the user.

The device implements a function returning an authenticating value, usually an encipherment, so that the device key and PIN are computationally unfeasible to derive without knowing the secret values and function concerned, using conventional cryptographic techniques. The host or agent performing authentication implements the same function, so that it may perform an equality test against the value returned by hand held device.

These types of device are capable of generating large authentication values, using encryption algorithms such as DES. However, since the user is required to enter the generated value onto a terminal keyboard (and a challenge value into the device in some cases), the range of values used is typically of the order of a five or six digit decimal number.

The functions used to generate the authentication parameter tend to make the values generated appear random, so that the values are effectively one-time passwords and are difficult to predict by an attacker.

Biometric Authentication Techniques

Biometric authentication techniques operate by measuring some physiological or morphological characteristic of the user. Wide interpersonal variations exist for most of the characteristics that may be measured, and including such characteristics as hand geometry, fingerprints and signatures.

Authentication is performed by requiring the individual to allow a measurement to be taken, and comparing the result of the test against a previously recorded profile for that individual. The profile may either be stored centrally, or on a security token presented at the time of authentication.

Biometric authentication techniques must cater for the natural variations that occur in the characteristics of every individual. Some mechanisms also experience practical difficulties in achieving accurate measurements, for example finger print images may be deformed due to smudging or distortion through unequal pressure. Biometric techniques are thus required to operate within tolerances hence an element of uncertainty is typically introduced into the authentication procedure.

The effectiveness of a biometric technique in authenticating identity for a known user population may be determined by conducting a series of trials.[87] In some cases, it may be that a certain number of authentication checks will fail, either accepting an impersonator or denying the authentic individual. The percentage of such failures are termed the *Impostor Pass Rate (IPR)* and *False Alarm Rate (FAR)* respectively. While it may be possible to adjust the tolerances of the biometric mechanism to reduce or eradicate one type of failure, this will tend to increase the incidence of the other type of failure, and a compromise tolerance may often be chosen.

A Metric for Comparing End-authentication Mechanisms

All end-authentication mechanisms return some type of information collected as part of the authentication procedure, be this in relation to something known, possessed or characteristic of the user. Although the nature of authentication parameters is extremely diverse, they may be compared by measuring the amount of information they collect and return, using an information theoretic approach.[88]

Information theory calculates information in terms of the probability of a particular message or symbol in the finite set of all possible messages of the same type. The application of this technique may be exemplified by considering password systems. User selected passwords tend to be easier for people to cope with, but are often highly predictable. System selection of random character sequences for use with passwords tends to dramatically increase the key space of a given length password, since user selection often chooses values from natural language. Natural language selections are limited by the strong statistical characteristics and structure exhibited by language.

For a natural language, structural dependencies exist at a variety of levels.[89]

- Zero order, individual letters occur randomly.

- First order, individual letters (symbols, or grams) occur with the expected frequency for the language.

- Second order (digram structure), each letter occurs with the expected probability, given its immediate predecessor.

- Third order (trigram structure), each letter occurs with the expected frequency given the immediately preceding digram.

– Fourth order, words occur with the expected frequency for the language.

– Fifth order, words occur at the expected probability given the preceding word.

The English language as an entropy per letter from approximately 2.3 bits per letter when 8 letters are known, to approximately 1 bit per letter when 100 letters are known.[90] The maximum entropy for a 26 letter alphabet is 4.7 bits per letter, demonstrating that natural language exhibits a high degree of redundancy. For example, a user selected eight character password may be expected to exhibit third-order characteristics (or above), and to have an entropy of around:

2.3 x 8 = 18.4 bits.

By contrast, a system selected (random) value would be expected to exhibit only zero order characteristics, and thus to have an entropy in the order of:

4.7 x 8 = 37.6 bits.

Further, common password values often occur with a high probability within the set of possible fourth order values, further reducing their information content.

Phonetic system selected passwords will have an increased tendency to exhibit second- or third-order characteristics by selecting pronounceable combinations of characters. As a consequence, the entropy will lie between those of completely random values and values selected from language.

Pass phrases[91] are measured in the same way, but exhibit characteristics of fifth order and above.

The use of information theory provides a general metric, applicable to other forms of authentication, and is capable also of modelling uncertainty and are vulnerability to compromise of authentication mechanisms.

Peer Entity Authentication

Computing systems may be formed dynamically from a collection of discrete components in a process known as binding. The components being bound may be, for example, mainframes connected by point-to-point high speed channels or personal computers connected to a local area network. Since only a loose logical connection may initially exist between the discrete components, from which a system is formed, the requirement for peer-authentication often arises.

The dynamic nature of computer networks and distributed systems places considerable dependency on the efficiency and effectiveness of authentication techniques. Typically these techniques are based upon symmetric or asymmetric cipher schemes, where the ability to perform a cipher transformation (ie possession of a secret key) constitutes a fundamental part of the authentication proof. A number of these have been introduced in the descriptions of distributed system mechanisms and protocols.

A number of techniques have been published.[92] The one described here is notable for the minimal number of messages sent between the parties involved.[93]

Assuming that system A and system B wish to establish a secure session between them. They intend to transfer sensitive data over an untrustworthy communication system, which they will protect using a symmetric encryption scheme. To establish their session they need to agree a secret session key and to assure themselves that they are conversing with the correct party.

The scheme that allows them to do this makes use of a trusted 'authentication server', which we will refer to as AS. Each system in the network has its own private encryption key, which is only ever known by itself and by the trusted server AS.

System A takes the initiative, and sends to B a message containing the following items:

1. A 'random' session identity, C.

2. A's name, A.

3. B's name, B.

4. A group of items encrypted under A's secret key, represented as:

    {IA,C,A,B}KA

The items are:

IA is a random value generated by A;

C is the value from (1) above;

A is A's name;

B is B's name.

{ ...}KA means the contents of the braces are encrypted using key KA.

When B receives this message it recognises it as the start of an authentication dialogue, but cannot decrypt it and has no assurance that the message really came from A (it could have come from an imposter). B constructs an encrypted group of items similar to that produced by A, but using its own random value (IB) and secret key (KB). It appends this to the end of A's message and forwards the whole to AS. The message now looks like this:

C,A,B,{IA,C,A,B}KA,{IB,C,A,B}KB

When AS receives this message, it can see that systems A and B are apparently trying to establish a session from the second and third fields. It then decrypts the encrypted parts of the message, since it knows the secret keys for both A and B. It can now compare the contents of the encrypted fields with those from the start of the message.

If the contents of the encrypted fields match, it accepts that the message must have been composed by A and B because nobody else could have performed the encryption correctly. Also, it knows from the C field and the names in the encrypted sections that it is not being presented with a forged message composed from recorded pieces of some earlier authentication exchange.

AS now generates a random session key SK, for A and B to use. It constructs the following message:

C,{IA,SK}KA,{IB,SK}KB

which it sends to B.

B recognises the value C and IB (which it recovers by decrypting {IB,SK}KB) and believes that the message came from the true authentication server because only it could have performed the encryption under KB. B sends the first part of the message (C,{IA,SK}KA) on to A. Similarly A is convinced that the message must have originated with AS.

Both parties are now in receipt of the key SK, and accept each others authenticity on the basis of the checks performed by AS. (Remember that they each included the (A,B) pair in their encrypted message to AS, stating who they wanted to communicate with and that AS was able to confirm that A and B were indeed involved in the dialogue based on their ability to perform encryption with the appropriate key).

Notes:

 1   Dei 84a p31, Pet 83a pp 10-13
 2   Tan 87a
 3   Sal 75a
 4   Fab 74a
 5   Fab 74a, Nee 72a
 6   Nee 72a
 7   Sal 75a
 8   Nee 72a
 9   Gra 68a
10   Gra 68a
11   Gra 68a
12   Sal 75a
13   Gra 72a
14   Gra 72a, Jon 79b
15   Gra 72a, Jon 79b
16   Jon 79b
17   Gra 72a
18   Sal 75o
19   Gra 72a, Pop 74a, Nee 72a, Lam 69a
20   Sal 75a
21   Sal 75a
22   Pop 74a, Jon 79b
23   Pop 74a
24   Pop 74a
25   Pop 74a

26 Nee 72a
27 Nee 72a
28 Jon 79b
29 Lam 69a
30 Jon 79b
31 Jon 79b
32 Lam 73a
33 Dod 83a, p79
34 Kem 82a
35 Den 82a
36 Den 82a
37 Riv 78a
38 Mey 82a, pp6-8
39 Fip 46a
40 Mey 82a, p162
41 Mey 82a, p162
42 Fip 46a
43 Mey 82a, p24
44 Coo 84a, p70
45 Fip 81a
47 Riv 78a
48 Jue 83a
49 Gif 82a
50 Den 82a
51 Koe 84a
52 Bar 84a
53 Per 82a, Woo 85a, Koe 84a, Bar 84a, Woo 83a
54 Mor 79a
55 Bar 84a, Has 84a
56 Has 84a
57 Bar 84a, Ber 84a
58 Ber 84a
59 Woo 77a, Woo 83a
60 Woo 77a, Sch 83a, Woo 83a, Ber 84a, Koe 84a, Woo 85a
61 Woo 85a, Mor 79a
62 Per 82a, Ber 84a
63 Sha 48a, Sha 51a
64 Woo 85a
65 Bar 84a
66 Woo 77a, Ber 84a

66 Woo 77a, Ber 84a
67 Woo 77a
68 Mor 79a, Woo 83a
69 Elk 84a, Mor 79a, Gal 78a, Eva 74a, Mey 82a
70 Lam 81a
71 Woo 83a, Woo 85a, Woo 77a
72 Woo 83a
73 Woo 77a, Woo 83a, Koe 84a, Woo 85a
74 Koe 84a
75 Ber 84a
76 Koe 84a, Woo 77a, Woo 85a
77 Woo 83a, Woo 85a
78 Por 82a
79 Fip 46a
80 Fip 81a
81 Por 82a
82 Bar 84a
83 Mor 79a, Woo 83a
84 Bar 84a
85 Bar 84a
86 Has 84a
87 Fip 48a
88 Osh 88a
89 Sha 51a
90 Sha 51a
91 Por 82a
92 Bir 86a, Nee 78a, Nee 87a
93 Otw 87c

(*see* Reference section).

5   Assurance techniques

5.1   INTRODUCTION

Assurance techniques attempt to convince the user that a system can be trusted to enforce the security requirements established for it. We will consider two of the more important techniques applied in the development and assessment of secure operating systems, avoiding an excursion into the general arena of program development.

5.2   PENETRATION TESTING

Penetration testing involves systematically attempting to breach the security of a system. In so doing it uncovers flaws in the system that may then be remedied.[1] A penetration exercise provides some indication of how resistant a system is to penetration, but ultimately does not prove that all flaws have been identified. Although penetration testing never provides absolute assurances, it is fundamental in all divisions of the TCSEC, and it is unlikely that any system with stringent security requirements would not be subjected to thorough penetration testing.

Penetration testing exercises have been extremely successful in locating security flaws in operating systems, to the extent that it was recognised early on that a reliably secure system cannot be built by relying only on penetration tests to locate flaws in it, since any determined attack might find previously unknown flaws. The extent and severity of flaws found by penetration tests suggests that systems built using casual development techniques are highly vulnerable to such attacks.[2]

The need for greater assurances resulted in the use of formal methods for the specification and implementation of highly secure systems. Through use of these techniques, the specification of a highly secure system is proved to be correct before its construction. These techniques are limited in terms of the size and complexity of system to which they may currently be applied. Indeed, implementation proofs are currently beyond the capability of the tools supporting formal techniques, and are not required even for the TCSEC A1 classification. In practice these limitations restrict the size and complexity of trusted software, but the assurance achieved through their use is considerable.

Penetration testing probably provides the highest degree of assurance attainable outside of the formal techniques applied to the development of highly secure systems. It is thus extensively used by the United States Department of Defense National Computer Security Center when evaluating systems according to the TCSEC. Penetration testing does not prove the absence of flaws, it only proves their presence.

The success of early penetration tests demonstrated the vulnerability of most general purpose systems, and showed that elimination of identified protection mechanism flaws provides only limited assurance that the security of a system is being improved. The elimination of one flaw often introduces another, particularly when the underlying problem is one of a design deficiency.

For the purpose of serious penetration testing, it is assumed that all relevant documentation and testing facilities are available to the penetrator. In particular it is assumed that a serious penetrator would have the opportunity to devise and test a penetration attempt on another computer of the same type. Thus a successful penetration would tend to be a swift and efficient operation, such that little reliance can be placed on detection of unsuccessful attempts through audit mechanisms (indeed a successful penetration would aim not to leave any obvious signs of either unsuccessful or successful attacks).

Penetration Testing Methodology

Early penetration testing exercises resulted in the development of a Penetration Testing Methodology.[3]

The methodology has four stages, these being:

- Gaining knowledge of system control structure during which the system in question is studied and understood in detail.

- Flaw hypothesis generation - likely areas of weakness are identified, and flaws postulated.

- Flaw hypothesis confirmation —flaw hypotheses are tested.

- Flaw generalisation — discovered flaws are generalised to help direct a search for similar flaws elsewhere in the system.

The methodology is iterative in that where a specific flaw can be generalised, an opportunity exists for exploiting other instances of the generic flaw, and further flaw hypothesis generation can take place. The four stages are covered in greater detail below.

Knowledge of System Control Structure

During this stage a period of study and analysis of the system is undertaken, involving the study of design documentation through to source code listings. The methodology uses control object dependency graphs as an aid to understanding the relationship between protected objects (termed 'security objects') and 'control objects' (such as the 'supervisor' mode bit) identified in the system. The control object dependency graph stands somewhere between an access control matrix model and an operating system flowchart, and tends to be hierarchic in nature.

Control object dependency graphs help to identify significant targets for attack, and also the implications of a successful attack on that object. Graphs from different penetration studies may be compared, to identify patterns of conceptually strong dependencies, such that deviation from conceptually 'strong' patterns may be indicative of a potentially flawed mechanism.

Flaw Hypothesis Generation

Flaw hypothesis generation identifies areas of the system where there is considered to be a high probability of a significant flaw existing. A number of clues pointing to potential flaws are:

(a) Documented bugs and warnings offer a potential area for exploitation, the inference being that the system is weak in such areas.

(b)   Functions that are seldom used or in some sense unusual are likely to be less well designed or validated than others, and thus relatively weak.

(c)   Control object dependency graphs may indicate overloaded or missing components (as above).

(d)   Specific attacks found to be successful in previous tests may be used to direct the search for potentially flawed areas.

Flaw Hypothesis Confirmation

This stage takes flaw hypotheses and tests their validity, ie it aims to prove or disprove the hypotheses. Once a flaw is located, a live test may be conducted to demonstrate its existence. Such tests are considered to be straightforward, although other tests require significant amounts of code; typically to perform initialisation of such mechanisms as I/O routines and the construction of timing tests.

Flaw Generalisation

Proven flaw hypotheses are often indicative of an underlying, generic weakness in the system. The purpose of flaw generalisation is to consider specific flaws to determine whether a generic weakness may exist. The result of generalising a flaw, for instance, may give rise to further flaw hypotheses in areas perceived to be dependent on the flawed component.

Generic Operating System Attacks

Penetration techniques found to be successful against a number of different systems are:

- Asynchronous attacks, for example when one process attempts to change the parameter values that have been passed to and validated by a procedure call in another concurrent process.

- Browsing for privileged or classified information within a system.

- 'Trojan Horse' attacks, involving the use of code with legitimate functions, but which in addition perform unauthorised clandestine operations.

- 'Error Inducement' attacks, that deliberately induce errors to exploit weaknesses in error handling environments, or to collect information returned by error handling routines.

- Where it is sometimes possible to attach to another user's interactive session in the period between that user disconnecting and the software or hardware acknowledgment of the disconnect request.

- 'Permutation programs' may be used to exhaustively test all possible values input to a function, the cited example being to test all possible permutations of primitive operation function codes in the search for undocumented or unintended primitive operations.

- 'Unexpected parameters', meaning to pass unusual or illegal parameter values (or combinations thereof) to privileged procedures, particularly through system calls, in order to search for flaws on the parameter checking of such procedures.

Penetration Testing and the TCSEC

The flaw hypothesis methodology is used by the NCSC during evaluation of a system. The size and experience of the penetration team involved is dictated by the division against which the system is being evaluated.

Evaluation at division C

For evaluation at division C, the penetration team comprises at least two people with first Degrees in computer science and the penetration exercise is conducted over a one to three month period. A minimum of 20 hours is spent running online penetration tests.

Evaluation at division B

For evaluation at division B, the minimum penetration team also has to include one person with a Masters Degree in computer science and at least one team member with previous experience of a penetration test on another system. The exercise is conducted over a two to four month period, and each team member must spend a minimum of 30 hours running online penetration tests.

Evaluation at division A

For division A, the team must include two people with Masters Degrees in computer science and at least two team members who have participated in penetration tests on another system. It is also required that the team include members capable of conducting and interpreting hardware diagnostic programs on the system and who are sufficiently competent to implement a device driver on the system. The penetration exercise is conducted over a four to six month period, with each team member conducting a minimum of 50 hours of online penetration tests.

Example Penetration Testing Exercise

An extensive folklore of operating system security flaws exists, but there is little detailed information available concerning the results of serious penetration tests. This is presumably so as not to publicise flaws. Further, many of the exercises will have been conducted by, or on behalf of government or military agencies and the results classified as confidential. As an example, we will consider the penetration exercise mounted on the Michigan Terminal System (MTS) at the University of Michigan, which succeeded in achieving total penetration of the system.[4] The MTS system was a binary privilege mode system run on an IBM S370 architecture. A common system segment is accessible only in supervisor mode, and each process has its own local user segment for non-privileged code and data. The successful penetration attacks were of the type described below.

The first type exploited authorised privileged routines to perform unauthorised operations, depending on the effects of incomplete parameter checking when parameters are passed to privileged routines by reference. This was exploited, to cause the privileged routine to overwrite an address parameter subsequent to its validation but prior to its use. The overwritten parameter was then used to obtain unauthorised access to the system segment since the parameter was not revalidated. Further, it was possible to select both the target location within the system segment and the value to be stored there.

A particular routine that allowed this to read input lines and returned the text itself, an associated line number and a character count for the line. A call to this routine could be constructed so that the return address for the associated line number, referenced the parameter supplying the address to which the character count was to be returned. By constructing a suitable file and reading the appropriate record from within that file, the routine would overwrite the character count return address with a line number chosen to correspond to a selected address within the system segment. The character count would then be written into that location. The value written to that location could be controlled (presumably within limits) by choosing the line length of the record being read. The principle of this type of flaw is illustrated in Figure 5.1.

5.3 FORMAL METHODS

Penetration testing in itself offers only limited assurance as to the security of a system, in that the failure of a penetration test does not conclusively show that the system cannot be penetrated by another team or with more effort. For highly secure systems this does not provide adequate assurance, and hence the TCSEC require the use of formal techniques in the design of systems for division A such as the Honeywell SCOMP system. Systems at division A are functionally equivalent to systems at level B3, and although more effort is expended on penetration testing during evaluation of a system at level A1, the primary difference is the formal techniques employed.

Formal methods are not widely used ouside of a few specialist areas, and most data processing staff are completely unfamiliar with them. Further, their relevance to contemporary operating systems is minimal, so we will settle for providing the simplest of overviews, hoping to give some idea of the way in which the need for high assurance through the use of formal methods tends to dictate many aspects of the design and development of secure operating systems. It should be recognised that there is a practical limitation on the assurance provided by formal techniques on systems of the size and complexity of operating systems. It is normally the case that the verification tools themselves have not been formally verified, often relying largely on investigation and user guidance for their successful operation.

A further area of concern arises from code compilers, where even if a language is amenable to code proofs, it is often the case that a large number of unverified library routines exist as a fundamental part of the language compiling system.

Protection system flaws of the type identified in the MTS exercise.

1. *the protected subsystem validates the addresses passed to it*

2. *one of the address fields is overwritten with an unvalidated value, which is then used to perform an unauthorised action at point 3.*

(Note that this type of flaw does not occur if the addresses are copied into local variables within the protected procedure prior to their validation and use. Similarly, the protected subsystem has no access to objects in the calling domain (except at CALL and RETURN time), such flaws are prevented).

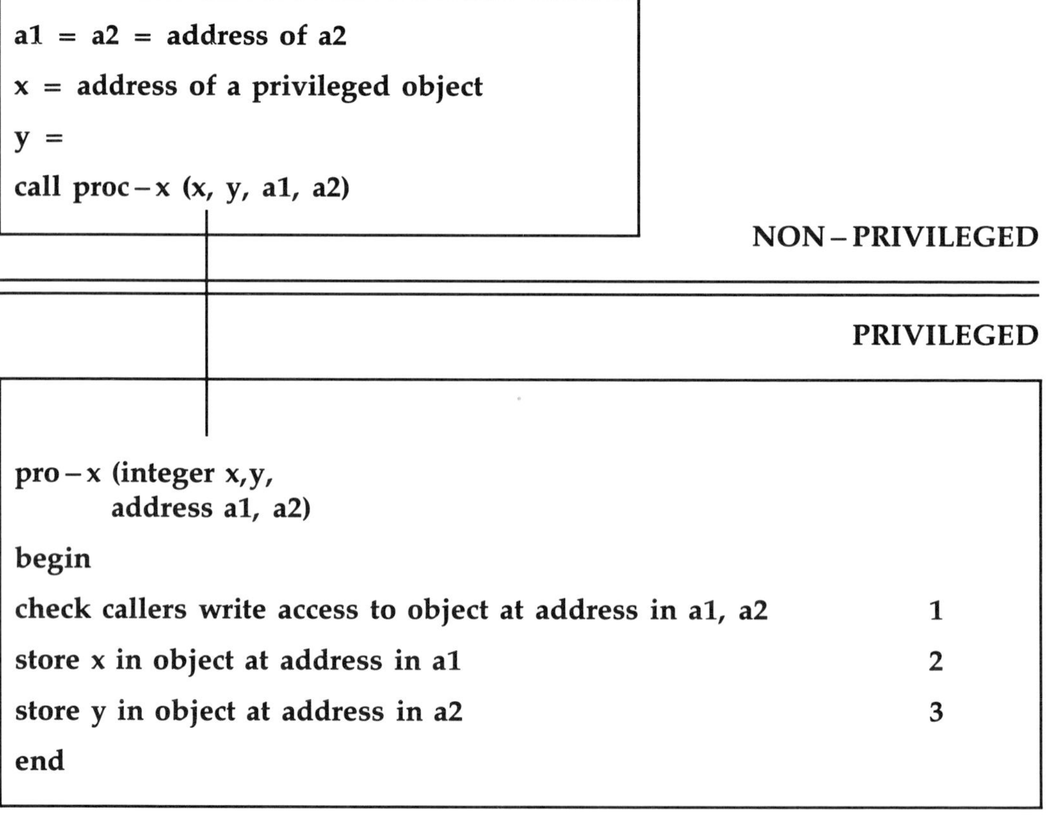

Figure 5.1 MTS Protection Flaw

For A1 systems, the TCSEC requires the production of a formal model of security (ie a formal specification of its security policy) in the system (Multi-Level Security (MLS) or a derivative thereof), and a Formal Top Level Specification (FTLS) of the interface to the TCB.

ITSEC also requires formal security policy models at the higher evaluation levels, but unlike the TCSEC is not prescriptive about the security policy being modelled or the specification system used. There is a marked preference for the Z specification method in the UK, while TCSEC evaluated systems have tended to use HDM or Gypsy. These have been described in public literature together with results of their use in secure operating system development, and it is these reports that are the basis for the following sections.

Formal Top Level Specification (FTLS)

The FTLS describes the interfaces to a security kernel and trusted software. Formal automated techniques are required to be used (should the appropriate tools exist) in proving that the security model is itself consistent and that the FTLS is consistent with the model. They must also be used to search for covert channels, although informal techniques are acceptable in the case of timing channels. Although formal implementation proofs are not required for A1 systems, informal techniques must be used to show the consistency of the FTLS and TCB implementation, and to show how the FTLS and TCB correspond.

Much of the effort of research projects in operating systems security has been expended on the development of formal techniques and the tools to support them. Secure operating systems were found to be considerably larger and more complex than software systems that had previously been developed using formal development methods, and most of the available methodologies and tools were severely limited for a task of this magnitude. The TCSEC requires that one of its currently approved formal methodologies be used for A1 systems.

Formal verification systems are generally hierarchic in nature, mapping high level abstract specifications down through a hierarchy of increasingly detailed specifications towards an implementation level.[5] Generally, the implementation level is a high level source language.

Hierarchical Development Methodology

The Hierarchical Development Methodology (HDM) was developed by SRI International, and had been used in the specification and verification of several kernelised operating systems. HDM is supported by languages and tools that aid the verification of multi-level security. It is limited in its ability to perform code proofs and verification of properties other than multi-level security.

There are two stages to the methodology:

- *Specification and verification* is concerned with the specification of the system as a hierarchy of abstract machines, and verification of the most abstract properties of those machines.

- *Implementation* is concerned with the correctness of the lower level abstract machines by which the verified, most abstract machine is implemented.

A system being specified in HDM is organised as a set of abstract machines. The highest of these describes the user interface to the system. Lower levels of abstract machine describe the system in greater detail, and are only available to the single abstract machine appearing directly above them in the series. Each abstract machine is specified as a set of modules in the HDM specification language, SPECIAL.

The Top Level Specification (TLS)

The most abstract of the machines specified describes the user interface to the system, and is often referred to as the Top Level Specification or TLS. The TLS is written in the specification language SPECIAL, and should be the simplest, most abstract description possible (undue complication in the TLS has been observed to considerably increase the difficulty in successfully verifying the TLS.) The TLS is the only abstract machine that is verified as conforming to a multi-level security model, and this verification is assisted by the MLS tool, which generates formulae stating that the TLS indeed conforms to the model. These formulae are passed to the Boyer-Moore theorem prover, and if they are indeed proven, then the verification attempt succeeds.

Security verification

Security verification in HDM is performed only on the Top Level Specification. Two tools are used in security verification, these being the Multi-Level Security Checker and the Boyer-Moore Theorem Prover. The MLS Checker performs information flow analysis on the TLS, and generates formulae that state that the observed flows are permitted under MLS.

Formulae that cannot be proven are indicative of either insufficient information available to the Theorem Prover, or of an information flow that is not permitted under the MLS policy. Trivial formulae, where the source and destination of a flow path are at the same security level, are resolved immediately by the MLS Checker. Formulae of greater complexity are passed to the Boyer-Moore Theorem Prover, together with information concerning MLS requirements, expressed in the LISP-like format required by the Boyer-Moore Theorem Prover.

The Multi-Level Security Checker (MLS)

The MLS checker works only for the MLS policy, and would have to be replaced by a similar tool if verification of a policy other than MLS was required. The TLS input to the MLS Checker requires that each function specified has a single security level associated with it. This is expressed as a parameter to each function, and the user of the MLS Checker must interactively identify which of a functions parameters is the security level. The user also expresses the ordering relation that exists between security levels. This technique allows the security level of a caller, external to the system, to be specified for calls made to functions in the TLS.

The MLS Checker generates a formula for each information flow channel that it detects.[6] Each formula takes the form of an implication, with the antecedent being the conjunction of all previously encountered flows, and the consequence being the information flow detected for the operation in question. Each flow is expressed in terms of the security levels of the information source and receiver, and is validated against the ordering relation supplied to the MLS Checker.

The formulae are generated strictly in sequence from the exception and effects statements given in a functions SPECIAL specification. The success of the verification attempt is dependent on the ordering of these statements, since it is necessary to ensure that all the flows are included in the antecedent of each formula generated by the MLS Checker. Thus, exception checks are specified to ensure the validity of information flow between objects of specified security levels. These exception checks are specified in the order in which information flows will occur.

Security verification

The verification of a system as complex as a security kernel is a considerably different proposition. In the case of SCOMP, the verification effort generated 2002 formulae, of approximately 100 lines of text each, although only 67 of these needed to be passed to the Boyer-Moore Theorem Prover.

In the case of the SCOMP system, 29 formulae were found to breach MLS by both manual inspection and by mechanical methods. A further four flaws were found by the mechanical methods only, and these were exceptional in involving more than three security levels. It is unfortunate, however, that the mechanical methods disclose only the presence of an illegal information flow, but do not determine its bandwidth (which may be tolerable) or its whereabouts.

The Gypsy Verification Environment

The Gypsy Verification Environment.[7] was developed at the University of Texas, and was intended to provide a complete environment for verification of both design and implementation. A single language, also called Gypsy, is used for both specification and implementation, with specification statements appearing interspersed throughout implementation code and certain statements, such as procedure headers, serving as both specification and implementation constructs. The Gypsy language is derived from the PASCAL programming language, with the addition of verification and concurrency constructs.

The Gypsy Verification Environment is based on techniques selected from the disciplines of structured programming, deductive proofs and formal specifications. Although it has no special tools for security verification, such as the MLS checker available in HDM, it has a selection of general purpose tools that may be exploited in the verification of security.

Specifications in Gypsy are essentially of two types.

- *External specifications* describe the externally visible characteristics and behaviour of an object. These specifications describe the interface to a routine, and the effect upon its parameters at various points in its interpretation. In particular, entry conditions and exit conditions are specified, together with hold conditions which must hold whenever a process blocks.

- *Internal specifications* are fundamental in implementation proofs. These specifications describe the internal mechanism of an object, ie the implementation detail which is not visible or detectable externally to the object. They include 'assert' statements which must hold at specific points in a routines interpretation, and 'keep' statements which must hold at all times.

Specification statements in Gypsy take the form of a Boolean expression, which may reference any number of constants, variables and functions. These statements may also include universal and existential quantifiers. When the Gypsy language is used throughout a system development, implementation consists of expanding Gypsy specifications with Gypsy implementation statements.

Implementation proofs using Gypsy are verified by showing that each routine satisfies an exit condition for both normal and exception cases. Verification conditions that aim towards this proof are produced by the Gypsy Verification Condition Generator, and are of the form:-

'entry condition + implementation code — exit condition'

These are then passed to the Gypsy Theorem Prover.

The Gypsy Theorem Prover is based on theories of natural deduction and first order logic. Typically, the Theorem Prover is invoked to prove a specific verification condition, and is guided throughout its operation by the user. In practice, the efficiency of the system is largely dependent on the direction provided by the user, and the user is often required to assist the Theorem Prover in proving apparently trivial theorems.

SCOMP Verification

For the verification of the SCOMP trusted software, specialised policies and models were defined for the security of the trusted software components.[8] These were necessary because much of the trusted software, by definition, did not strictly conform to the MLS policy. Three policies were defined as being applicable to the SCOMP trusted software (and possibly to trusted software generally), although not all the policies would be applicable in every instance of trusted software. The policies defined were:

1. A privilege policy.

2. An integrity policy.

3. Functional correctness policy.

The privilege policy

The privilege policy controls the use of the three privilege types associated with invocation of certain kernel functions, modification of security attributes and the ability to override kernel security policy. The latter type tends to be required when a function must read and write data at different security levels, or when a trusted path into the kernel is being supported.

The integrity policy

The integrity policy is concerned with operational and administrative controls rather than information controls. It is applied to restrict certain functions to users authorised for their use. The SCOMP integrity policy defines the ordered set of integrities as USER   OPERATOR   ADMINISTRATOR.

The correctness policy

The correctness policy is concerned with those functions whose correct operation is critical to the security of the system, even though the functions concerned may not be privileged under either the privilege or integrity policies. Such functions may be subjected to particularly thorough analysis, since implementation verification is typically still impractical.

Conclusions from the SCOMP Verification

A number of observations were made following the experiences of the SCOMP verification effort for its kernel and trusted software.[9]

It was observed that although the manual verification techniques resulted in detection of most design errors (essentially covert channels), complex errors were discovered only by mechanical techniques. The interdependency between manual and mechanical techniques was found to be extremely close, with the success of mechanical efforts largely dependent on preceding manual analysis. While mechanical verification was successful given sufficient attention to the specification style rules and conventions required by the verification tools, the results of mechanical verification required careful manual analysis to determine the location and implications of the detected flow. In many cases the detected flows were within the allowed bandwidths, or did not in reality represent any potential security flaw.

The SCOMP kernel was specified in 3300 lines of SPECIAL, representing about one man year of effort. By contrast, the kernel was implemented in approximately 10,000 lines of PASCAL code and required about nine man years of effort. Of the 33 unprovable verification formulae detected by automated techniques, 29 had already been identified by manual inspection of the specification. In fact, all of the detected flows were acceptable. It was observed that even for the kernel, strict adherence to the MLS policy (as verified by mechanical techniques) was not a realistic expectation for a practical system. The trusted software verification was complicated by the lack of a covert channel analysis tool, so that this analysis had to be performed manually. Further, implementation was performed in the C programming language, and the manual mapping between Gypsy specification and C source code was complicated by the relative abstraction of the Gypsy TLS, compared to the C implementation code.

Notes:

1   Lin 75a
2   Att 76a, Heb 80a, Wik 81a
3   Lin 75a
4   Heb 80a
5   Che 81a
6   Silv 83a
7   Che 81a

(*see* Reference section).

6 Secure operating system architectures

6.1 INTRODUCTION

This chapter looks at operating system designs and architectures that have proven to be the most suitable for implementing highly secure operating systems. Most of these are of a type known as Security Kernels, although distributed systems are appealing because the physical separation between components can result in simplification of the other protection mechanisms required.

Security kernels are a strict implementation of a reference validation mechanism. They are significant because they demonstrate the limits of our ability to construct secure operating systems and because they identify the practical problems, constraints and trade-offs that purely theoretical studies might fail to recognise. In the case of distributed systems, certain communication paths will be provided over a network instead of being internal to the Security Kernel, and suitable mechanisms must be deployed to protect them.[1]

6.2 SECURITY KERNELS

A security kernel is responsible for enforcing a security policy, as opposed to merely providing a set of protection mechanisms.[2] The kernel Multics and KVM/370 projects demonstrated that much of the complexity and function found in the most primitive domains of a conventional operating system, could reside in less privileged domains.[3]

In a security kernel, all security critical functions are implemented within the kernel, and functions not critical to security are excluded (as far as is possible). This is a requirement of systems being evaluated at level B3 of the TCSEC, which requires the use of a security kernel design. The kernel itself is kept as simple as possible, so that its specification may be subject to verification (the limitations of verification techniques being a major constraint on kernel specification and design).

The architecture of a kernelised operating system is typically layered. The kernel is normally the lowest and most primitive level. The structure and much of the function of a conventional operating system environment is implemented above the kernel, and a typical structuring has at least kernel, supervisor and user layers.[4] The requirement to minimise complexity in a kernel leads to attempts to implement as much function as possible in higher level layers. Conversely, the requirement to include security critical functions within the kernel may result in it implementing some security functions that would normally be provided by higher level components in a conventional system.[5]

Function

The primitives implemented in a kernel are minimal and the range of object types supported may be fixed or variable (if object types may be dynamically defined). Equally, the number of objects of a given type may be fixed or dynamic.[6] Object types frequently exported by security kernels are:

- Processes[7];

- Segments[8];

- Capabilities[9];

- Devices or I/O services.[10]

If sufficient function is excluded from the kernel, it is possible for the kernel to provide little more than the implementation of primitive abstract resource types, with all kernel functions (including those invoked by interrupt) being allowed to run to completion.[11]

Hardware

Kernel design and performance can be greatly assisted by suitable hardware support.[12] This is exemplified by the Honeywell SCOMP and SAT systems, which both aim for high degrees of assurance, and both of which have exploited specialised hardware.

The SCOMP system runs on a modified minicomputer, using standard peripheral hardware,[13] with the addition of an extra hardware module called the *Security Protection Module (SPM)* between the system processor and the other functional units. The SPM mediates individual accesses to objects, using virtual addresses and capability-like objects called descriptors. Descriptors are constructed by the SCOMP kernel following validation of an access request, and are organised into a hierarchic structure. Enforcement of access control was placed in hardware to reduce the overhead incurred in earlier systems such as KVM/370 and KSOS. It was claimed that these had delivered only 10-25 percent of the usable processing power of a conventional operating systems running on the same hardware.

The principal design concept of the SAT is that of a kernelised reference monitor.[14] It aims to simplify the verification of its reference monitor while achieving acceptable performance, by implementing the reference validation mechanism primarily in hardware. This simplifies its verification, allowing simpler and more convincing arguments that its reference validation mechanism is tamper-proof and cannot be by passed. The SAT runs on specialised hardware, with a co-processor used to implement the additional operations of the reference validation mechanism. In general, four hardware features have been specifically identified as useful in the implementation of security kernels.[15]

First, support for multiple processes, with efficient context switching and IPC primitives.

Secondly, a large segmented virtual memory system providing variable size segments. This provides efficient support for protecting the implementation of many objects within the system. The kernel is typically responsible for creating and managing segment descriptors, including access control and label fields, which the hardware then uses when mediating access to a segment.

Thirdly, a minimum of three hierarchic execution domains is useful. If only two domains are available, the result is likely to be inefficiency due to overloading the user domain with conventional operating system functions, since the kernel alone would use the most privileged mode.[16]

Fourthly, adequate control over the effects of I/O operations. Normally, I/O operations can be initiated only from within the most privileged (ie kernel) execution domain. Device and I/O handling accounts for much of the complexity of kernels.[17] I/O requests are passed to the kernel by non-kernel software, which the kernel validates before executing. An alternative is to provide a descriptor type object, constructed by the kernel and referenced by the hardware, that may be associated with I/O requests originating from non-kernel software. Such a scheme requires hardware (or microcode) support, but offers improved performance since the kernel need not provide mediation for all I/O operations.

Since a security kernel is usually implemented at the most primitive level of the operating system architecture, it is normally responsible for many aspects of hardware interfacing and control. The diversity of device types and the cleanliness of their interfaces largely determines the complexity of the software required to support them. For example, many channel devices are not subject to address translation, operating on absolute addresses in both primary and secondary memory, and the kernel may need to compensate for this lack of protection.

Performance

Performance requirements may also influence the complexity of a kernel by introducing more sophistication and limiting the migration of function out of the kernel.[18] For example, the complexity of the Multics most privileged ring was excessive, due to the need to avoid ring switches on the early systems in which these were handled by software.[19]

Security Kernel Architecture

The architecture and structure of the kernel is influenced by the overall architecture of the operating system. In particular, the issue of whether the kernel runs 'in-process' (within the address space of user processes) or out of process (separately from user processes) can be significant. In the first case the kernel data structures are shared between processes, in the latter case they may be isolated from user processes and the kernel may not run in a normal process environment at all.[20]

The architecture of a kernel will normally be better structured than that of a conventional operating system supervisor, as its components and the relationships between them will have been subjected to much greater design rigour and formality.[21] This may result, for example, in the kernel running in fixed memory locations to avoid both complexity and the awkward relationship that often exists between memory and process managers.[22] It has been noted however, that error handling can be a particularly awkward issue to resolve. Where possible, concurrency will be excluded from the kernel in the interest of simplicity and ease of verification. This may require that kernel primitives run non-preemptively, whether invoked by higher level software or by hardware (as a result of interrupts).[23]

Resource Management

A major function of a kernel is likely to be resource management. The desire to remove unnecessary function from the kernel results in consideration of whether some aspects of resource management may be shared between the kernel and higher level software. A likely effect of hierarchic structuring is that the higher level resource pools are effectively partitioned by the constraints placed on the underlying primitive resource types. Partitioned resources will in general be less utilised. Even for the minimal set of resource types implemented by the kernel, it is possible to further reduce kernel complexity by moving the mechanisms responsible for the management of those resources outside of the kernel. A clear example is in the case of the memory management process often found in operating systems, whose responsibilities (for example) might include making swapping decisions which the kernel executes.

A related issue concerns naming, since names are themselves a type of resource. It is usual for high level names to be mapped onto lower level names, for example a filename may be mapped onto block cache names. Responsibility for name management and name mapping within the kernel tends to be restricted to primitive naming schemes.[24]

Trusted Software

The majority of kernelised systems have implemented certain privileged functions in trusted software outside of the kernel. In principle, the kernel implements access control and information flow control between the objects that it implements in keeping with the security policy it is required to enforce. Trusted software provides services to applications running above the kernel, or implements functions that would complicate or prevent the verification of the kernel.[25] It is trusted in that it either provides services that are critical to the security of the system, or it is privileged to override the general security policy in some specific way.

Examples of functions implemented in trusted software are:

- Sign-on and trusted path services[26];

- File system support[27];

- System operator services[28];

- System maintenance services[29];

- System administration services.[30]

Since trusted software is often in breach of the kernel security policy, the policy governing privileges must be supplementary to the general kernel security policy, and high levels of assurance are sought for trusted software functions. Typically, the policy defined in respect of trusted software will be specific to the type of function being performed, unlike the kernel security policy which is usually general. The specialised security policies defined for trusted software in the SCOMP are a good example.[31]

File Systems

In some cases, a kernel or trusted software may export a simple file system, typically limited to flat file structures.[32] The simplicity of these, and that of the associated naming system, are such that higher levels of software are then used to construct a more abstract file and naming system. The complexity and hierarchic structure of these higher-level mechanisms, and the close relationship between protection and naming, prohibits the provision of such systems directly from a kernel.

6.3 DISTRIBUTED SYSTEMS

Consistent definitions of distributed systems are given in the literature.[33] In essence they agree that the presence of multiple processing nodes and interconnecting communication services should be transparent to the users of the system. This contrasts with network operating systems, where the topology of the computing system is directly apparent to users, such that individual nodes and the resources they support are typically referred to directly. The treatment in terms of security, presented below, does not significantly differentiate between distributed and networked operating systems. In this respect, the term 'distributed' is intended to cover both types of system.

A distributed system may be defined as one where discrete components of processing activity occur in more than one processing node of the system, at one or more physical locations or where explicit communication is required between discrete components of the system.[34] It has been observed that an inherent consequence of distribution is that of separation between discrete components of the system; specifically that this separation allows the use of isolation or interlocks as a method of security policy enforcement.

Several properties of distributed systems directly assist the construction of secure systems:

- Many of the system components are distinct, and the separation between them clearly defined.

- Communication channels between such components are clearly defined.

- Components typically implement only a limited, specialised set of functions.

These observations have resulted in interest in distributed systems as the basis for constructing and modelling secure systems,[35] and may allow separation and mediation requirements to be treated separately.[36] While mediation will require some form of trusted entity within the system (normally TNIUs with a limited number of specialised servers), a primary advantage of a distributed system is that it may exploit several types of separation mechanism, namely physical, temporal, cryptographic and logical (eg using separation kernels). Trusted nodes, typically servers of some kind, often exist in secure distributed systems, providing such services as multi-level file systems, print servers, authentication servers and key servers. Because the function of servers is usually specialised, their security policies may be degenerate and thus easier to specify and enforce.

Such specialisation of function and security policy has an analogue in trusted software in security kernel systems, evidenced by the special policies verified for the SCOMP trusted software.

Remote Procedure Call

Remote Procedure Call (RPC) is an important technique in distributed operating systems whereby procedures located on different processors on a network may interact using a high level mechanism that preserves the semantics of a local procedure call.[37] The transport protocols most suited to RPC favour simplistic but efficient connections of short duration. The brevity and frequency of RPC connections is such that connection establishment costs, handshaking, state retention costs and any other unnecessary protocol overheads must be minimised.

A conventional RPC protocol is often therefore of a connectionless nature, such that arrival of a request is sufficient to establish the necessary state information in the server without the overhead of any preamble. Such state information may then be deleted after a suitable period of inactivity.

Early research work on RPC was extended to consider issues of security. The objective was to design and implement a secure RPC service providing peer-entity authentication and message authentication.[38] The secure RPC service exploited conventional communication security techniques and mechanisms. Peer-entity authentication was based on the Needham/Schroeder scheme while DES in CBC mode was used for message confidentiality and integrity with each participating system having a private DES key. The secure RPC service is interesting due to the requirement for light weight, efficient end-to-end communication with minimal state information retained in RPC server systems.

The concept upon which the secure RPC service was founded was that of a 'conversation', which equates to a cryptographic session between two principals (ie a client and server system). An authentication server is responsible for managing the DES keys of the other systems in the network.

When a client system wishes to establish a conversation with a server system, it must obtain authentication data and a conversation key to present to it. These are obtained from the authentication server using a key known only to the client and the authentication server. The authentication server returns a conversation key and an 'authenticator', which is a data object that a client can present to a server as proof of identity. The authenticator contains the client name and the conversation key, and is sealed under the server's secret key. Both client and server systems retain information pertaining to conversations in an RPC run time support data structure indexed on conversation-id. In the case of clients this is initialised as part of the authentication dialogue with the authentication server. Servers may discard information relating to a client (and hence conversation) after a period of inactivity (although never in the middle of a multi-packet secure call, since otherwise a replay attack could cause the call to be executed twice). Servers need to acquire the necessary information to support a conversation in a secure and efficient manner.

When a server receives an RPC packet containing a conversation-id that it does not recognise, it stores the packet and returns to the client a *'Request for Authenticator' (RFA)*packet, which includes a timestamp. On receiving an RFA packet, the client RPC runtime system will generate and return a 'response to RFA packet' which includes an authenticator and the encrypted time-stamp.

Separation Kernels

The separation of components in a distributed system has the advantage that interaction between components has improved visibility and is easier to control. A practical limitation may arise if the number of logical units required is greater than the number of physical units available. A mechanism for resolving this is a 'separation kernel'.[39]

A separation kernel constructs and maintains a set of virtual environments abstracted from the available physical resources. A separation kernel is intuitively similar to a Virtual Machine Monitor, and is required to implement a virtual environment which cannot be distinguished from the real environment by software running above it. It differs from a Virtual Machine Monitor in that it is not necessarily required to provide an exact copy of the real architecture and in that it must provide a mechanism allowing communication channels to be implemented between software objects running in separate virtual environments. This simulates the discrete components of a distributed system environment.

Complications occur because in the absence of real protection mechanisms (eg a real TNIU), the separation kernel must enforce the legality of communications. It is unclear how the separation kernel could allow a multi-level trusted object to transmit (downgraded) data at a security level less than the upper bound of all data it had been observed to read, unless the security kernel recognises that the object is trusted. It might be simpler to use separation kernels to support multiple objects of a single security level, protected from objects at other security levels by, for example, a real TNIU.

A Multi-level Secure File Server

A distributed system that enforces multi-level security suffers from a considerable drawback when a lower level entity legitimately wishes to send information to a higher level entity. A distributed system would normally require the receiving entity to acknowledge the receipt of such information to assure its correct delivery and indeed a mandatory integrity policy may demand that this be done. This acknowledgement would be prohibited under an MLS policy since it constitutes an information flow from a high to a lower security level. This differs from information flow between entities in a centralised system in that the integrity of the transmitted data is usually ensured using protocols that require two-way message transfers.

One solution to this problem implements all such communication through a secure file server, in units of UNIX files.[40] Communication is achieved by a lower level entity sending a file to the secure file server, with the secure file server acknowledging its receipt. The second stage of the communication is initiated by the higher level entity, which requests a copy of the file from the secure file server. (An alternative would be to use an NTCB partition in each hardware node. This could assume responsibility for delivery of the data which it performs transparently.)

The organisation of the secure file server minimises trusted components by using a single trusted reference monitor (SFM) to control a number of untrusted, single-level file servers. The SFM is accessed via a TNIU, which is capable of handling multiple encryption keys (since traffic to the SFM will be encrypted using a key associated with a particular security level). The SFM is trusted to direct data to the correct single-level file server. The SFM is responsible for ensuring that the untrusted file servers cannot breach security policy. This is achieved by attaching a cryptographic checksum (such as generated by DES in CBC mode) to each file before sending it to the untrusted server for storage.

The checksum is generated to include the filename and timestamp, using an encryption key associated with the security level of the file concerned, preventing the untrusted server from returning the wrong file. Since the SFM mediates all LAN access by the untrusted servers, with TNIUs protecting and enforcing direct communication between the SFM and the untrusted servers, the SFM is capable of ensuring the integrity of all files returned by untrusted servers by recalculating their checksums before transmitting them over the LAN.

The cryptographic separation achieved, between files at different security levels in this scheme, allows the use of multiple untrusted servers (ie one per security level) to be relaxed. An alternative organisation uses a single untrusted file server attached to the LAN, with a TNIU ensuring that only the SFM can communicate directly with it (their TNIUs sharing a unique session key). The SFM provides mediation in all access requests to the untrusted server and uses cryptographic separation to enforce security policy within the untrusted server. An interesting aspect of the scheme is its dependency on an implicit integrity policy for protecting the labels, names and contents of files.

Notes:

1 DoD 87a, ISO 88a
2 Ame 87a
3 Sal 74a, Sch 77a, Gol 79a, Gol 84a
4 Pop 79a, McC 79a, Ber 79a, Gol 79a, Gol 84a, Gra 83a
5 Pop 79b
6 Sch 77a, Fei 79a, Fra 83a
7 Pop 79a, McC 79a, Ber 79a, Fra 83a
8 Pop 79a, McC 79a, Ber 79a, Fra 83a
9 Pop 79a, McC 79a, Ber 79a, Fra 83a, Fei 79a
10 McC 79a, Ber 79a, Fra 83a
11 Pop 79a
12 Sch 77a, Pop 79a
13 Fra 83a, Ben 85a, Sil 83a
14 Boe 85a, Boe 87a

15 Ame 87a
16 Gol 79a, Gol 84a
17 Pop 79a
18 Pop 79b, Gol 79a, Gol 84a
19 Sal 74a, Sch 77a
20 Pop 79b
21 Sal 77a, Sch 77a, Gol 79a, Gol 84a, Pop 79a
22 Pop 79a, Sch 77a
23 Pop 79a
24 Pop 79b
25 Pop 79a
26 Pop 79b, McC 79a, Ber 79a, Fra
27 Pop 79a, Fra 83a
28 McC 79a, Ber 79a, Fra 83a
29 McC 79a, Ber 79a, Fra 83a
30 McC 79a, Ber 79a, Fra 83a
31 Fra 83a, Ben 85a
32 Fei 79a, Pop 79a
33 ANS 87a
34 ANS 87a
35 Rus 81a
36 Rus 83a
37 Bir 84a
38 Bir 85a
39 Rus 81a
40 Rus 83a

(*see* Reference section).

7   Examples of contemporary general-purpose systems

7.1 INTRODUCTION

We have already considered much of the background to secure operating systems; now it has to be considered how effective contemporary systems are in this area.

As soon as we start to consider specific, individual systems, much of the theory and concepts become blurred under the confusing mass of details and features that characterise each different system. We should not be dismayed by this, for the concepts we have discussed can be readily identified without too much effort, once we understand what to look for. Equally, we cannot ignore the detail of each specific system. On the contrary, we must be prepared to investigate and understand the implications and nuances of the features and mechanisms concerned. The suppliers documentation is almost always the most reliable source of technical information, and one should not hesitate to familiarise oneself with this.

To help illustrate the sort of detail involved, and to shed some light on the types of security weaknesses often found in contemporary systems, we will consider two examples:

1. MVS, developed by International Business Machines for use on their large-scale mainframes and those of compatible hardware suppliers. Although MVS is often criticised for the antiquity of its design, it supports a large range of applications software and accounts for the majority of large-scale systems throughout the world.

2. UNIX, developed originally at Bell Laboratories, but now the subject of intense interest as a vehicle for providing 'open systems' and as a multi-

tasking operating system for powerful microcomputers, minicomputers and workstations.

Commercial systems such as these are typically limited to divisions C and D of the TCSEC, and security is not normally the most important of their design requirements. The general increase in security awareness, encouraged somewhat by a desire among suppliers for their products to achieve a respectable TCSEC certification, has resulted in a trend of enhancing the security features of existing commercial systems. The recent efforts made in producing or enhancing optional 'security' packages for the systems above should, therefore, be interpreted as a trend rather than a coincidence. Examples of these developments are the recent certification of MVS/ESA to level B1 of the TCSEC, and AT&T's commitment to achieving B2 of the TCSEC, with UNIX System V Release 4 Enhanced Security. The POSIX Security Extensions bear witness to a commitment to operating systems security on the standards front.

Correctness and Integrity of OS software

A major consideration for all the systems reviewed concerns the correctness and integrity of the operating system software. In large systems particularly, the operating system software is often subjected to extensive and frequent patching to remove errors. Further, it is often possible to customise these systems by including third-part product modules into the operating system, or having user-written modules invoked as 'exits' or 'hooks' from system code to achieve particular effects. In this respect each instance of some large operating systems should rightfully be considered as unique, and certifications awarded to such systems treated with caution (since each may have a different TCB in the terms of the TCSEC).

The variations and instability of large system implementation must be contrasted with the verified design and rigorous implementation techniques of highly secure systems. The reason for using formal techniques in highly secure systems is the assurance of correctness and impenetrability provided. In practice the supplier of a large system can only offer limited assurances concerning these properties, examples being:

(a) A commitment to rectifying any flaws that are discovered in the primitive protection mechanisms upon which the systems security depends and in the use that an operating system makes of these primitives. Clear examples of this are provided by the 'statements of integrity' made by IBM in respect of the MVS and VM operating systems[1].

(b) The wide exposure that some large systems achieve may result in increased confidence that fundamental flaws will have been detected and rectified.

(c) Certification, currently to some level of the TCSEC or ITSEC.

System Configuration and Access Controls

In addition to issues of correct design and implementation, a fundamental concern for commercial systems relates to system configuration and access controls. Typically, commercial systems provide discretionary access controls and primitive end-authentication mechanisms (ie passwords). If these are not carefully established and maintained, then breaching the systems security may become a facile activity (as evidenced by most of the 'hacking' reports found in the press).

Most widely used systems have well known, standard objects that are critical to the systems security (such as the libraries containing operating system code modules) and standard privileged user names (such as: SYSTEM, MAINT or SUPER.SUPER). Adequate access controls must be established to protect critical objects, and adequate end-authentication mechanisms (typically passwords) must be applied to privileged users. These requirements are often accomplished manually, and depend upon the diligence of responsible staff for their maintenance. In reality this responsibility is subject to the inherent fallibility or lack of awareness of the individuals concerned, and lapses in this area (particularly with poor choices of password for privileged users) account for the majority of the system penetrations reported in the press. These limitations are prevalent in most commercial systems of the TCSEC division C category. They meet the division C criteria only when properly configured and maintained, and thus are properly described as having the potential of achieving division C certification. These systems differ significantly in terms of their structure and primitive mechanisms, not having been developed with the unifying objective or disciplines apparent in highly secure systems.

Comparisons between these systems and the highly secure systems surveyed previously must be made judiciously. The highly secure systems are all of a much smaller scale than those of this chapter (recall that SCOMP was developed originally as a front-end communications processor for MULTICS). Even at this reduced scale of size and complexity, numerous trade-offs arise between issues of security, function and performance. In a relatively small and specialised system, reductions in function and performance for the sake of security may be acceptable. By contrast, much of the emphasis and motivation in large systems is related to the need for the provision and continual expansion of very large scale application systems. In these circumstances there is often little or no latitude for reductions in function and performance, limiting the compromises that are acceptable.

These difficulties appear to limit the usefulness of large systems for handling information of high security levels, or information at different security levels. Techniques such as the use of secure systems for controlling data flows into and out of large systems appear to provide a possible solution for large scale applications that have significant security requirements.

7.2 MULTIPLE VIRTUAL STORAGE (MVS)

Multiple Virtual Storage (MVS) is IBMs largest operating system, used on its large mainframe systems and those of it's major 'plug compatible' competitors. MVS thus supports a large percentage of the worlds large computing systems, as indeed it has done over the last decade and will continue to do so for the foreseeable future.

MVS has its origins in the IBM operating systems of the 1960s. In particular, the MVT (Multi-programming with Variable number of Tasks), together with optional features such as the Time Sharing Option (TSO) and Job Entry Subsystem (JES2 or JES3, descended from the Houston Automatic Spooling System and the Automatic Spooling System respectively) are clear ancestors of MVS.

Versions of MVS

There are several versions of MVS. Those used currently are MVS/XA and MVS/ESA. The differences between these two versions are minor as far as their main security features are concerned.

MVS was first released in 1974, although many of its features and structures have their origins in the MVT (Multi-processing with Virtual number of Tasks) operating system dating back to 1967.[2] In many respects the design and implementation of MVS reflect the state of the art in system engineering as it existed in the 1960s and the need to preserve compatibility between MVS and software developed for earlier operating systems has resulted in a commitment to structures and techniques that are undesirable and over-complicated by contemporary standards.

The MVS System

MVS uses a two-state protection system, this being the limit of the System 370 architecture. Access control and authentication mechanisms within MVS are minimal, and are typically augmented by the use of 'security packages' which are invoked by MVS internally. Resource protection is provided by MVS, and IBM have issued a statement of integrity, for MVS, which is a commitment to provide features within MVS that allow secure systems to be implemented.[3] The statement of integrity represents an undertaking by IBM to provide sufficient mechanism within MVS to allow an installation to control the use of privileged process states, address spaces and storage protection keys within the overall system.

The issued MVS system can be, and very often is, modified and augmented by third-party products and by system programming staff at customer installations. Such alterations to the functions provided by MVS may be implemented in a variety of ways, including modification of the issued source code, implementing code invoked by MVS at standard 'exit' points and provision of additional features such as 'user defined' system calls.

Although a standard MVS system with an access control package can attain a level of C2 security rating and even B1 in the case of MVS/ESA, the security achieved at any given installation is critically dependent upon access controls and any modifications made to the basic system. In most cases, alterations to MVS functions are made in assembler level code, such that the scope for introducing security flaws is considerable.

The progression of MVS

The ancestry of MVS accounts for most of its remarkable characteristics. Most of the current knowledge concerning construction of large computer systems, and operating systems in particular, was not available in the early 1960s. Many of the data structures and interfaces today that would be invisible outside of the operating system itself (or more precisely, outside of a subsystem or object within the operating system), were visible to application code and directly accessible. These structures and interfaces thus became fixed by the dependency that many large customer installations developed on specific implementation details. Indeed, the distinction between operating system and application was eroded in many cases, and it is still common practice for software packages to supply system call handlers, that will be included in the operating system under the provision of 'user supplied' system calls. Ultimately the rigidity imposed on internal details of the operating system mechanism places considerable restrictions on the designer and implementor of the system in that existing details cannot easily be changed and parallel structures may need to be established should the original become inadequate (disk space management being an example, using Volume Table of Contents (VTOC), VSAM Virtual Data Set (VVDS), Syscat, VSAM catalog and ICF catalog data structures).

MVS is undoubtedly the most popular operating system on large mainframes. The continued commitment to old data structures and interfaces also means that MVS continues to support a wealth of software developed over the years. It also means that competition by software developers and hardware suppliers is possible, so that the overall investment in MVS and related software is immense.

System 370 Architecture

The System 370 architecture provides the protection primitives for operating systems such as VM/SP and MVS/XA. An understanding of its features is a prerequisite to understanding the security of those operating systems.

The Program Status Word

The Program Status Word (PSW) holds processor state information. Fields within the PSW contain:

1. The program counter;

2. A field used to select virtual or real addressing modes;

3. A bit used to enable (or disable) interrupts for I/O, program exceptions, machine check (hardware) and certain user selected interrupt types (such as arithmetic exceptions);

4. Condition code bits;

5. The current value of the storage protection key;

6. The processor state bit, selecting supervisor or problem state;

7. The wait state bit, used to halt further instruction interpretation pending an interrupt.

The PSW is not directly addressable, but is updated via privileged instructions (the Load PSW, LPSW instruction) or by hardware.

Storage Protection and Page Protection

Storage protection is implemented by the System 370 architecture using protection data associated with each 4K page of real memory. The protection key associated with a page frame is compared with the protect key field of the Program Status Word. Several possibilities exist:

– If the PSW protect key is 0, then the request is (assumed to be) a privileged component of the operating system, and the request is allowed to proceed.

– If the PSW key and page protect key are equal, the request is allowed to proceed.

– If the PSW key and page protect key are unequal, then requests to store into the page are failed. Requests to read from the page depend on the fetch protect bit, also associated with each page by hardware (this is the only time the fetch protect bit is used).

Instructions modifying the page protection data (Set Storage Key Extended — SSKE) are privileged within the System 370 instruction set.

In addition, the hardware supports a feature called 'page protect' used to prevent a page from being modified, irrespective of protect key assignment.

Page protection is controlled by a protect bit set in page table entries, and is typically used to prevent overwriting of critical re-entrant code areas within operating systems.

Addressing

The hardware supports the use of both real addresses and virtual addresses under the control of the 'translate' bit in the PSW. Real addressing will usually be restricted to components of an operating system. Such components may alternatively use privileged instructions (Load, Real, Address) to access real memory.

Virtual addressing

Virtual addressing is the normal mode used, and implements multiple address spaces using a paged segmented scheme. Virtual addresses occupy a 32-bit word, within which addresses may be 31 or 24 bits. The address size is selected by the high order bit (selecting 31-bit addressing when set) in an address word. The use of 24-bit addressing is the original system 370 mode, with 'extended architecture' machines and operating systems increasingly making use of the 31-bit address format.

The 31-bit virtual addressing scheme provides a 2048 megabyte virtual address space, comprised 2048 segments of one megabyte each, with each segment containing 256 pages of 4K bytes each.

Virtual addresses are translated directly by hardware, although segment and page tables are constructed by software. The real address of the current segment table is loaded by software into the primary Segment Table Origin field in control register 1.

Segmentation and page tables

A segmentation scheme is used, but is degenerate in that the majority of segments will have the same properties and segmentation is used largely as a technique for limiting the size of page tables. Segment table entries contain a 26-bit page table origin, a segment invalid bit, a common segment bit and a four bit page table length field. Segment tables are allocated at their full extent to occupy two contiguous pages of real memory.

Page table entries may be dynamically allocated as required, such that the space occupied by page tables may be limited. Page table entries contain a 19-bit real address of the corresponding real page frame (if allocated), a page invalid bit (if no real page frame is currently allocated) and the page protection bit.

Control registers

Fourteen control registers are defined in the architecture. These are used by hardware, microcode and software for a variety of purposes, several of which are fundamental and critical to security. The instructions available to software for addressing the control registers are all privileged, allowing retrieval of control register contents by the STCTL (Store Control) instruction and modification of control register contents by the LCTL (Load Control) instruction. The registers of particular significance to security are:

- *Control register 0*: This contains fields controlling address protection, dual address space control and virtual address translation.

- *Control register 1*: This contains the length and starting (real) address of the current address space segment table.

- *Control register 3*: This contains a PSW mask used in cross memory services, and the identity of a secondary address space used in cross memory services.

- *Control register 4*: This contains a bit mask used to increase storage access privileges when using cross memory services and the identity of the primary address space when using cross memory services.

- *Control register 5*: This contains the starting address and length of a linkage table used in satisfying program calls between address spaces as supported by cross memory services.

- *Control register 7*: This contains the length and starting address of the segment table of the secondary address space used in cross memory services.

Processes

The concept of a process does not appear in MVS literature. Each of the address spaces supported by MVS is represented by an Address Space Control Block (ASCB) and the despatcher maintains and searches (in priority order) a queue of ready ASCBs when selecting a 'process' to despatch. Within a ready address space, a hierarchy of 'tasks' may exist, representing programs being executed, one or more of which may currently be despatchable. Having selected an address space, the despatcher searches the queue of despatchable tasks in priority order.

There are thus at least two interpretations of the concept of a 'process' in MVS:

1.   A process is an address space, within which multi-tasking may occur (similar to the concept of light-weight processes on some other systems).

2.   Processes are tasks, which may share address spaces.

MVS itself uses discrete address spaces to implement certain functions (*see* Figure 7.1) and it appears to be a current trend to move functions from common memory into such system address spaces.

In addition to the address space and task mechanisms, MVS uses another type of despatchable entity called a Service Request Block (SRB) for activating system services on behalf of applications. Service requests may be global, in which case they are despatched in advance of any address space, or local, in which case they are despatched ahead of any despatchable tasks in the address space with which they are associated.

Protection Keys in MVS

MVS uses the storage protection key feature of the System 370 architecture in the following way.

–   *Key value 0* is used only by the MVS supervisor. All critical operating system areas and shared code ('link pack') areas use a page protection key of 0.

–   *Key value 1* is used by JES, and to protect pages in the Scheduler Work Area (SWA).

–   *Key values 2, 3 and 4* are not currently used, but are reserved for future use.

Master Scheduler	Address space creation and deletion
PC/AUTH	Authorisation and linkage tables for cross-memory services.
TRACE	Tracing of MVS activity.
GRS	Resource locking services based on resource name.
Dump services	Performing diagnostic dumps.
Catalog	Cached access to file catalog structures.
Console	System operator communication.
ALLOCAS	Resource allocation services.
SMF	System Management Facility logging.
JES2	Job Entry Subsystem.
LLA	Link List Lookaside, cached look-up services for link-list modules.

Figure 7.1 Examples of MVS/XA System Address Spaces

– *Key value 5* is used by data management routines, providing file access facilities such as opening and accessing files.

– *Key value 6* is used by the Virtual Telecommunications Access Method (VTAM), providing network access and management functions.

– *Key value 7* is used by the Information Management System (IMS), providing database and transaction processing facilities. IMS runs with

protection key 7 to exploit functions of system macros that test for
storage protection key values of less than 8.

–   *Key value 8* is the standard key value used by applications running under
     MVS.

–   *Key value 9 through 15* are used by applications that require to use real
     addressing to carry out specialised functions such as translation of
     channel programs. When running in real addressing mode such
     applications are not separated by the virtual addressing mechanisms, but
     may use different storage protection key values to prevent access to each
     other's memory, (*see* Figure 7.1).

MVS Virtual Storage Organisation

Virtual storage organisation under MVS reflects the separation of operating
system and application programs, and an evolution from 24-bit addressing to
31-bit addressing (*see* Figure 7.2).

Components of the Common Area appear at the same virtual address in all
address spaces, such that MVS code and data areas may be shared, and
allowing the sharing of data areas between address spaces. Components of the
Local Area may differ in every address space.

The 24-bit virtual addresses used in the original System 370 architecture have
influenced the structure of the current system, with many components residing
at addresses of less than 16 megabytes (the limit of the 24-bit address space).
To exploit 31-bit addressing, the organisation above the 16 megabyte address
boundary mirrors the organisation below that address, with system code and
data gradually being moved above the 16 megabyte virtual address boundary
as part of maintenance and development of the MVS product.

The Structure of MVS/XA Virtual Address Spaces

Common areas are equivalent in all address spaces. The structure below 16
megabyte addresses is that of the original MVS/370 system, which used only
24-bit addressing. The MVS/XA system retains compatibility with MVS/370
applications by maintaining the original structure below addresses of 16
megabytes.

2046Mb	**Extended Local System Queue Area** **Extended Scheduler Work Area** **Extended Authorised User Key Area**	**Extended Private Region**
	Extended User Region	
	Extended Common Service Area **Extended Link Pack Area** **Extended System Queue Area** **Extended Nucleus**	**Extended Common Area**
16Mb	**Nucleus** **System Queue Area** **Link Pack Area** **Common Service Area**	**Common Region**
	Local System Queue Area **Scheduler Work Area** **Authorised User Key Area**	**Local Region**
	User Region	
0	**Prefix Save Area**	**Common Region**

Figure 7.2 MVS/XA Virtual Address Structure

The Common Area: The Common Area includes all objects that must appear at the same virtual address in more than one address space. This includes much of the MVS code and many of its data structures.

The Nucleus: The MVS Nucleus includes the primitive MVS functions supporting processes (address spaces), virtual memory and I/O abstractions. It is located immediately above and below the 16 megabyte virtual address, occupying around one megabyte of virtual memory. The Nucleus runs with locked pages, and includes the hardware configuration data structures which are merged into the Nucleus area during system initialisation.

The System Queue Area (SQA): The SQA holds transient data structures required by the MVS operating system. Its size is established during system generation.

The Link Pack Area (LPA): The LPA holds modules containing code that implement MVS functions outside of the Nucleus, but may additionally (and often does) contain other modules of pure (re-entrant) code. There are three subdivisions of the LPA. The *Fixed Link Pack Area (FLPA)* holds modules requiring fixed pages (typically because they cannot tolerate page faults), the *Modified Link Pack Area (MLPA)* is pageable and contains modified versions of modules from the *Package Link Pack Area (PLPA)*. The contents of the LPA are established from a parameter file (in the standard SYS1.PARMLIB library) searched during system initialisation. The modified LPA is reloaded with each IPL, whereas the PLPA image is stored for re-use across different IPLs. The MLPA is typically used for testing or introducing modifications to modules located in the PLPA, and is always searched before the PLPA.

The Common Service Area (CSA): The CSA is used to hold objects that must appear between address spaces, and is used to support high bandwidth inter-process communication. It is heavily used by the VTAM subsystem for buffering. The granularity of storage key protection limits use of CSA for secure inter-process communication, in that programs from any address space may access the contents of CSA provided they have the correct PSW key loaded.

The Prefix Save Area (PSA): The PSA occupies the low order page of virtual memory. The PSA contains fixed locations used by hardware, and is frequently used for communication between hardware and software.

The Private Area: The private area contains those areas of local scope within an address space. Below the 16 megabyte address boundary approximately four to five megabytes are available for user programs, with the remainder of the private area being used for local objects maintained by MVS on behalf of the address space and the programs executing within it. These local objects are:

- The Local System Queue Area (LSQA), holding local control blocks.

- The Scheduler Work Area (SWA), containing control blocks used by JES within the address space.

- The Authorised User Key Area (AUK), holding objects used within the address space protected by a storage protection key — typically used by data management (for example, DBMS) routines running within the address space.

Authorised Programs

Certain functions provided by MVS are security or integrity sensitive, and their availability must be restricted. The concept of 'authorised programs' is adopted in MVS, such that only authorised programs may invoke sensitive functions.

An authorised program is one that satisfies at least one of the following conditions:

- The program is executing in supervisor state;

- The program is executing with a PSW protection key value of less than eight;

- The program is executing as part of an APF-authorised job step (a bit known as JSCBAUTH in the Job Step Control Block (JSCB) being set on).

The Authorised Program Facility (APF) is the mechanism used to obtain privilege for application or installation written system code. For MVS to treat a program as APF authorised, several conditions must be met:

- The first module loaded must have the 'authorised' property set, either by the linkage editor (using the 'SETCODE AC(1)' statement) or by the Job Control Language statements used to invoke the first module (the statement PARM='AC=1,...' appears in the JCL);

- All the modules invoked were loaded from 'authorised libraries';

- No unauthorised libraries were searched in satisfying external references from the original module.

Since no controls are normally placed on the ability to set the authorised property bit in code modules, control of the authorised program facility (and thus overall security and integrity of the MVS operating system) ultimately depends on access controls protecting authorised libraries. The authorised libraries are defined by parameter files accessed during MVS initialisation and by MVS standard conventions. The conventions ensure that essential MVS libraries are considered to be authorised in all cases, these being:

1.   SYS1.PARMLIB, used to hold parameter files accessed during system initialisation.

2.   SYS1.LPALIB, containing code areas loaded into common areas, this library only being considered authorised when accessed during system initialisation.

3.   SYS1.LINKLIB, containing generally available code modules, and any libraries considered as logical extensions to the LINKLIB as nominated in the LNKLST file within SYS1.PARMLIB.

This scheme does not require that modules other than the first have the authorisation code set, on the assumption that all code paths have been validated from such a module, when invoked as the first in a job step, to all other modules called from authorised libraries. In addition to the standard libraries, an arbitrary set of libraries may be authorised via parameter files interrogated during system initialisation. The parameter files concerned are held within the standard MVS library SYS1.PARMLIB, being the IEASYSxx and IEAAPFyy files, where xx is specified by the system operator during IPL and yy is specified by an APF=yy statement within the IEASYSxx file.

A statement within the IEASYSxx file effects the nomination of authorised libraries, and may take the form LINKAUTH=LNKLST or LINKAUTH=APFTAB. In the former case (the default) all the libraries concatenated to SYS1.LINKLIB (the 'linklist') are treated as authorised (these are nominated in the SYS1.PARMLIB *(LNKLSTnn)* parameter file, and are searched by the loader as a logical extension of SYS1.LINKLIB). In the latter case, the linklist members are not automatically authorised, and authorised libraries are explicitly nominated in the SYS1.PARMLIB *(IEAAPFyy)* file. Entries in the *(IEAAPFyy)* file give a library name and a volume serial number, to prevent users from creating a library with the name of an authorised library, but on a private volume.

The principal method of establishing and maintaining control of authorised programs is thus control over access to authorised libraries and those parameter files that identify authorised libraries. MVS provides two mechanisms allowing code to establish whether its caller was an authorised program.

First, if the code is invoked by system call, the system call can be defined such that it will only succeed when issued by an authorised program (FC01 parameter, as opposed to FC00 is specified on the system call definition in the SVCTABLE macro during system generation, allowing protection to be enforced by the system call interrupt handler). Secondly, the code may use the TESTAUTH system macro, which indicates whether its caller was authorised.

Certain MVS routines treat APF authorisation as different from supervisor state or protection key value of less than eight. Such routines may restrict facilities from callers that are only APF authorised. In the event that JCL is used to concatenate a non-authorised library into an authorised library, both libraries are treated as non-authorised for the duration of that job step.

The types of functions available under APF authorisation include page fixing and the ability for a module to change its mode to supervisor mode and its storage protection key value to a value between 0 and 7 (the MODESET macro being provided to facilitate these operations).

The System Authorisation Facility (SAF)

The System Authorisation Facility (SAF) provides a common centralised interface definition for use by MVS subsystems or applications responsible for the management and access control of resources. The component of SAF that provides this interface is called the MVS router. Subsystems controlling resources may invoke a 'security' package (such as the IBM RACF product, or the Computer Associates ACF2 and Top Secret products) over the SAF interface at key points (called 'control points') in their processing, in order to use the user authentication, resource access control or audit functions of the package.

Standard macro instructions are provided that allow subsystems to exploit the SAF interface, in particular the RACROUTE macro. The RACROUTE macro may in turn invoke the RACHECK or FRACHECK macros to pass requests to the security package. On return from the RACROUTE macro, the contents of a general register indicate that the request was authorised (value 0), that the request could not be serviced for such reasons as the security package not currently running (value 4), or because the request was not authorised (value 8).

The Program Properties Table

The Program Properties Table is held in the Extended Common Service Area
(ECSA) and identifies program modules that require special properties during
execution, and specifies the properties concerned. The majority of these
specialised properties afford a program some degree of privilege within the
context of the MVS environment, hence the acquisition of these properties
must be controlled. The mechanism whereby programs may execute with
special properties are specified by a SCHEDnn file within SYS1.PARMLIB,
where nn is specified in the SYS1.PARMLIB[7] file selected for the current
session. The SCHEDnn file is read during system initialisation, and is used to
build entries within the Program Properties Table. Entries within the
SCHEDnn file identify programs by name, and for each program specify the
required properties using parameters from the following set:

- **CANCEL** or **NOCANCEL**, indicating whether program execution can be
  abandoned by the system operator.

- **KEY(n)**, where n specifies the storage protection key value that the
  program will execute under.

- **SWAP** or **NOSWAP**, used to indicate whether the address space running
  the program is swappable.

- **PRIV** or **NOPRIV**, indicating whether the program is privileged, in
  which case it will only be swapped if the program is in a long wait
  condition.

- **DSI** or **NODSI**, indicating whether normal file integrity (ie potential
  concurrent update condition) checks are to be applied at the time the file
  is opened.

- **PASS** or **NOPASS**, indicating whether normal file access control checks
  are to be applied or not. These checks include native file password checks
  and calls to a security package if present.

- **SYST** or **NOSYST**, indicating whether the program represents a single
  step system task, in which case it may be started directly by the system
  operator using a START or MOUNT command.

Components of MVS

This section presents an overview of the primary functional components of MVS/XA.

The Job Entry Subsystem (JES)

There are two alternative versions of JES, known as JES2 and JES3. Their differences are insignificant in this context, largely limited to differences in the way resources are assigned to jobs and the way multi-processor configurations are supported. The JES subsystems are the primary means of job input and output in MVS. Jobs are input to MVS through terminals, card readers, remote job entry systems or a program interface known as an 'internal reader'. These jobs are expressed in Job Control Language (JCL), which is a syntactically primitive language describing a job in terms of programs called, files accessed and input and output data streams.

The System Management Facility (SMF)

SMF maintains log files containing events of some significance as notified by the various components of MVS. It constitutes an important audit file from a security point of view, although records written to the SMF log files are often highly structured and require interpretation. Some access control packages log information into the SMF log files, as well as or instead of into audit files of their own.

The Time Sharing Option (TSO)

TSO provides an interactive environment for terminal users. Each user of the TSO service is attached to a different dedicated address space, and may submit commands or invoke C-lists (a simple interpretive language) directly. Typically TSO is used to support the Interactive System Productivity Facility (ISPF), which offers a more powerful, menu-driven user interface.

Users logging on to TSO are defined in the standard SYS1.UADS file, which contains the user identity and a lists of their TSO privileges (such as the ability to call MVS operator commands and the ability to define new TSO users).

System Calls

System calls are invoked by the SVC instruction, which takes as an operand, a value between 0 and 255 identifying a particular system call. The range of values between 0 and 199 is reserved for use by IBM, but values in the range 200 to 255 are available for customer use. Thus the range of system calls available may be extended, typically in support of database management or transaction processing systems. Restrictions placed on the system call mechanism preclude its use in a cross memory environment, when MVS locks are held, when the processor has been disabled for interrupts (signified by a bit in the PSW) or when the processor is running system routines scheduled as an SRB (System Request Block).

System calls cause an interrupt which is handled by the system call first level interrupt handler. This enforces certain restrictions on system calls, dependent on the type of system call involved, and passes control to the routine for handing the particular system call in supervisor mode with a protection key of 0.

System calls are of six types. The differences between types concern:

–   Whether the SVC routine is resident in the nucleus or the PLPA, which is largely concerned with its pageability.

–   Whether the SVC routine is to run enabled or disabled for interrupts.

–   Where the current processor state information is to be saved on entry to the SVC routine.

–   Whether the SVC routine itself can issue further system calls.

–   Whether the local lock (essentially a mutual exclusion semaphore) may be held on entry to the SVC routine.

The properties of the six available SVC types are shown in Figure 7.3. Type 5 is a null type, used primarily as a place holder, and the reasons for the existence of the identical types 3 and 4 are now entirely historic, dating back to the MFT era.

The system calls available in the user defined range (200 – 255) are defined in the IEASVCnn parameter file within the system parameter library

SVC Type	Nucleus resident	PLPA resident	Interrupts enabled	Can issue SVC	Can hold local lock
1	yes		yes		yes
2	yes		yes	yes	optional
3		yes	yes	yes	optional
4		yes	yes	yes	optional
5					
6	yes				

Figure 7.3 MVS/XA System Call Properties

SYS1.PARMLIB. The contents of this file are used during system initialisation in the construction of the SVC Table, interrogated by the system call first level interrupt handler. The contents of the SVC Table may be dynamically changed by code running in supervisor state with a storage protection key of 0, and the SVCUPDTE macro is provided to facilitate this feature.

Properties of MVS/XA system calls (SVCs) for the six different types of system call defined.

User Exits

To enable great flexibility and customisation of MVS without requiring modification of MVS code, a number of 'user exit' points are provided. These are points in MVS control paths at which user written routines may be invoked, which allow data structures to be interrogated or modified, or for normal logic decisions to be influenced or overridden.

User exits are implemented in the following ways:

- By replacing a 'null' module provided as part of the standard product.

- By providing a list of standard exit point names in the initialisation parameters (often held in a file in the standard SYS1.PARMLIB library), which will cause a module of a predefined name to be invoked at the appropriate point.

- By providing lists of modules (with arbitrary names) in initialisation parameters, each list associated with a specified exit point, each member of which will be invoked in the specified order.

A typical example of the use of user exits is to validate JCL statements for parameter ranges or conformance to local standards, or to provide default or override values to certain parameters.

Many users exits are invoke from privileged code, and receive control in supervisor mode with a storage protection key value of zero (from which supervisor state can be achieved if not already set). Like user written system calls and APF authorised programs, user exits introduce a considerable element of uncertainty into the security and integrity of an MVS system. The components of MVS and related software products that offer user exit points include JES, TSO, SMF, BCP, DFP, RMF, VSAM, VTAM, RACF (or equivalent product), HSM and IPCS. Most of these offer several exit points, totalling over a hundred exit points between them (*see* Figure 7.3).

MVS Access Control Packages

A number of commercial access control packages are available for the MVS operating system. These packages do not protect anything, that is the responsibility of the software that manages each given resource type (for example, MVS itself manages files), to which end the resource manager may use the protection mechanisms provided by the hardware to separate the resources from the entities that require access to the resources. The access control packages provide user authentication, access authorisation and audit trail functions to the resource managers, although the resource manager is not required to make use of these facilities.

Many software products provide mechanisms of their own, since there is no guarantee that an access control package will have been installed, but many packages can use an access control package instead of their own native mechanisms. The advantages of doing so are that the task of administration is made simpler, and the native mechanisms of many packages are either crude or in conflict with mechanisms used by other software products (for example, the existence of multiple sign-on mechanisms using different identities and passwords for the same user weakens an already unreliable authentication scheme).

It is important to recognise that use of the SAF is optional, and that protection of resources is the responsibility of individual resource management subsystems using the architectural protection primitives. Hence the presence of an access control package does not always imply an increase in security in that the system is not necessarily less vulnerable to penetration. Access control will normally be better co-ordinated by use of an access control package, although many software products that exploit privilege within the context of the MVS operating system choose to use an access control mechanism of their own rather than use the SAF interface — for example, the Spool Display and Search Facility (SDSF) product marketed by IBM uses data structures defined by macro expansion and assembly of loadable object code modules.

MVS packages in common use

The three MVS access control packages in common use are:

1.   Resource Access Control Facility (RACF) from IBM.

2.   Access Control Facility 2 (ACF2) from Computer Associates.

3.   Top Secret from Computer Associates.

These packages are similar in concept, although implementation details differ. All recognise resources by name, and allow access control decisions to be based on pattern matching operations between resource names and character masks. The functions they provide for user authentication are all similar, including password management based on such factors as minimum password length, password lifetime and validation of user selected passwords to prevent use of words that are too easy to guess. All the packages provide audit trails using SMF (although Top Secret recommends the use of its own mechanism instead of SMF) and reporting programs for analysing this data.

Each package provides some concept of 'privilege' that can be associated with given user identities. This usually means that the associated user has the 'right' to override the access rules that would otherwise apply. Control of such 'privilege' is clearly important as 'privileged' users can easily compromise TCB integrity, for example, by accessing operating system libraries. Examples of such privilege are:

-   *SPECIAL* on *RACF:* providing the ability to change RACF access control data;

-   *OPERATIONS* on *RACF:* providing the ability to override normal access rules;

-   *SECURITY* on *ACF2:* providing the ability to set ACF2 access rules;

-   *NON-CNCL* on *ACF2:* providing the ability to access resources for which permission has not been granted by ACF2;

-   *NODSNCHK* on *Top Secret:* meaning that access rules for files will be ignored for this user-id (ie access will be granted).

Discretionary security is provided in respect of the TCSEC, although each package is aiming at mandatory security to B1 level (IBM are leading the way with RACF 1.9, the others are bound to follow because they must compete on an equal footing). They all allow the discretionary aspect of security to be controlled in the sense that the ability to define access rules is usually limited to a small number of individuals (often a small, central department is set up purely for this purpose). The term 'discretionary' is somewhat misleading in this respect, as most large organisations use these products in a manner that lies somewhere between the notions discretionary and mandatory, as defined earlier.

The packages recognise an 'owner' for most of the resources familiar to them. In most cases the 'owner' of a resource is a user or a group of users, and the resource is often generic, for example, in the sense that it is 'all files whose name begins with the characters SYS1'. The 'owner' of a resource is allowed to access it, but is not necessarily allowed to grant others access rights.

All packages allow the structure of the organisation, using it to be modelled, and for access rights to be mapped against this model. In practice this proves to be the approach adopted by most large commercial organisations.

RACF

RACF was the first of the access control packages to be released for use on MVS, being developed and supported by IBM. Software products interface with RACF through a number of standard system calls:

- *RACINIT:* This is used to check a supplied user identity and to verify the password supplied by the user. If successful, RACF constructs a data structure (known as an ACEE) in a protected area of memory that is used when validating subsequent access requests.

- *RACHECK:* This is used to check whether a request for access to some specific resource should be granted. The software controlling the resource passes the name and type of the resource, and the mode of access requested to it, as parameters to the system call. The ACEE is used to obtain the user identify, and a return code indicates whether the access should be allowed.

- *RACDEF:* Used to update data in the RACF database.

- *RACLIST:* Used to construct a cache of RACF access rules so that subsequent access checks can be performed with greater efficiency (usually used in transaction processing systems such as CICS).

- FRACHECK: Similar to RACHECK, but referring to cached data obtained through RACLIST.

- RACF maintains a database holding information about resources, users and access rights that have been defined to it, and it inspects this data to determine the appropriate respnse to give to the various SVCs above.

- RACF models organisation structure using a network of 'groups'. Groups may be connected to other groups, and users may be connected to groups. Granting access rights for an object to a group grants that access to all the users connected to that group. Users may be connected to groups with certain privileges, for example, to allow them to control access to resources owned by the group (or any of its subgroups) or to connect additional users to the group.

ACF/2

ACF/2 was originally developed by SKK Inc to compete with the early version of RACF. It competed extremely well as the early RACF versions were rather crude and many sites found them unacceptable or too inefficient. ACF/2 was, therefore, the choice of many of the early large MVS installations and, of course, once implemented in a complex site it is likely to remain there.

ACF/2 works by placing 'intercepts' in existing code, which then communicate with ACF/2 using SVCs defined for that purpose. It stores access rules in 'logon-id' records and in rule sets. A logon-id record describes a user, and a rule describes which logon-ids may access the resource associated with the rule.

Rule sets are usually generic, in the sense that the SYS1 rule applies to all files whose name begins with SYS1. They are normally entered in text form using an editor and must be 'compiled' into the ACF/2 database. They can be decompiled subsequently, but any annotation is lost. Perhaps the most distinguishing feature of ACF2 is the way in which users are associated with rules and the way that organisation structure can be modelled. Both of these are achieved using string matching techniques.

A string called the *UID string* is defined during ACF/2 installation, the structure of which is always the same. Typically the last section of the string is the user identity (known as a 'LID'), and the earlier parts are used to capture organisation structure. For example, suppose a company was organised into three divisions, called A, B and C and each division was then split into four departments, called 1, 2, 3 and 4. If each user is to sign on with a four-character identifier, the structure of the UID for that organisation could be:

    VDLLLL

Where V is the division, D is the department and LLLL is a user's log-on identity.

For example, user FRED in division B, department 3, might have a UID of:

    B3FRED.

ACF2 rules typically refer to UID values rather than user identities, and wild card characters are provided. For example, if a rule allowed read access to a file to all UIDs with a value of *3****, it would apply to all users in department 3 of all divisions.

A users UID value is defined when the user is declared to ACF/2. UID strings also allow administrative domains to be defined using a technique known as 'scoping'.

Top Secret

The Top Secret access control package is the most recent of the popular MVS access control packages, developed in the early 1980s. It runs within each user address space in protected storage and within a dedicated system address space managing and providing access to its database, with communication between the two achieved using the 'standard' RACF type SVCs.

At the start of a user session, a capability list for the user's protection domain is constructed from the database and loaded into LSQA, within the user address space. Access control decisions can then be made without further database accesses. Access control information for globally accessible objects (the ALL record in Top Secret) is stored in the SQA area.

Top Secret represents objects, both users and resources, as records in a database it maintains.

Active Objects, that is the principals using the system, are represented by an Access Control Identifier (ACID), which typically has its name on the users logon identity for TSO originated jobs.

Each user of the system is represented by a user ACID record, which is used to record the users' password, administrative authority and a list of object names and access rights forming a capability list for the user. In addition to user ACIDs, there are department, division and profile ACIDs. Department and division ACIDs are used to group user ACIDs into a hierarchy for the purpose of administration, allowing administration of the user population to be devolved to divisional and departmental user ACIDs. Profile ACIDs are used as a convenient mechanism for granting common sets of access rights to a number of user ACIDs. Access rights may be granted to a profile ACID, and the profile then added to the capability list of appropriate user ACIDs, granting access to the objects appearing in the profile ACID.

A special case of an ACID is the ALL record, with object accesses granted to the ALL record being globally available without otherwise needing to be defined for specific user or profile ACIDs.

Passive objects are associated with user ACID access lists by name. Matching the use of wild-card characters is provided, so that resources with similarly structured names need not be identified individually. Object ownership is not necessarily conferred to the creator of an object, but rather is conferred down the user ACID hierarchy from the root user ACID, known as the Master Security Administrator (MSCA). This ownership of resources is specified using the same naming conventions as for access lists and often resources are owned by department or division ACIDs.

The *types of object* represented within Top Secret include 'facilities' (TSO, CICS, batch jobs and started tasks), files, disks, tapes, libraries, operator commands and user defined resource types. The access modes vary with the resource type, but for example file access modes include read, write, update, create, purge and fetch (execute). Further, access may be granted only between selected dates and times and only from jobs running or submitted from selected terminals.

Administrative privileges are required by those user ACIDs that create and maintain user ACIDs within a department or division. These privileges are devolved through the organisational hierarchy from the MSCA, and are limited in scope by the position of the ACID concerned within that hierarchy. Administrative privileges are required to perform such actions as user ACID maintenance, audit functions, transfer of object ownership and the granting of access rights to objects. Rights transfer often involves co-operation between two administrative ACIDs, the first creating a profile and releasing to all administrative ACIDs (the GAP attribute), the other adding the profile to the access list of the user ACIDs within its scope. Note that there is no way to selectively release the ability of administrative ACIDs to confer access to resources, so that all administrative ACIDs are essentially trusted in this respect.

MVS Configuration Control

MVS requires careful attention to be paid to its control if any lasting assurance of security is to be maintained. There are a large number of configuration options that are important to preserving its TCB integrity and for supporting any higher level security mechanism that may be required (such as databases or transaction monitors).

Several of the important aspects involved in maintaining control of an MVS system are:

1. Control over access to the build materials from which a usable copy of MVS is constructed (source code libraries, macro libraries, job libraries etc). Much of the system generation process is controlled using the SMP/E software tool, which is used to manage the application of software maintenance and to control much of the system generation process. The SMP/E product and the files it uses require protection against alteration.

2. Control over access to the SYS1.PARMLIB library, which is used to specify load-time configuration options for MVS. In practice this is how most of the locally configurable controls over MVS are exercised. This library contains a hierarchy of parameter files which control a wide variety of options. It is described in more detail later.

3. Access control of privileged code libraries. There are a number of standard libraries, such as SYS1.LINKLIB and SYS1.LPALIB, which are used to contain modules that appear in the link list and link pack area respectively. These standard libraries can be supplemented by others specified in members of the SYS1.PARMLIB library. Of considerable interest is the member that specifies the libraries that form the APF list.

4. Contents of privileged code libraries. The fact that privileged code can alter most of the available memory means that it can by-pass TCB controls, and alter the TCB code or data directly. In fact many third party products do precisely this, changing standard MVS code or data to achieve specific effects that support the function of the product. Typically, the product is installed in an APF library with the claim that 'no modifications' are required to install the product, but as soon as the initial program is executed from the APF library it makes all manner of alterations to the MVS TCB. In practice most installations accept this in all innocence, because they are not aware of it happening. In reality however, at least one of the commonly installed products is reputed to contain a diagnostic trap door sufficient for complete compromise of the

TCB, and clearly any assurance afforded by MVS security evaluation is sacrificed.

5.   Control of operator commands and job entry (JES) subsystems. MVS and various of the subsystems it supports provide the system operator with control commands that allow it to be dynamically controlled. The ability to submit commands can be permitted to users other than system operators, often unintentionally due to poor configuration controls. A related issues (because it concerns job entry subsystems) is job input from 'RJE' or networked JES systems (running on separate MVS systems). It is not uncommon for connected JES systems to 'trust' each other, which means that compromising one of the systems exposes the connected systems since jobs can be transmitted from one to the other (with forged user-ids, etc).

The area of most practical interest for those concerned with security in MVS is the SYS1.PARMLIB library. Files within SYS1.PARMLIB are all character files, and all have eight character names. The first six characters identify the purpose of the file, with the last two characters forming a suffix by which different versions of the file are identified. In all cases the suffix '00' acts as a default value.

The file IEASYS00 is used when MVS is loaded to select which of the other files will be used. This itself is a default, as the system operator can specify a different suffix in reply to a prompt issued during system initialisation.

Within IEASYS00 are entries that define which suffix to use in selecting other members of SYS1.PARMLIB to be used. For example, an entry of 'APF = AA' would select the file IEAAFPAA to be used instead of IEAAPF00. If there is no entry for a particular PARMLIB member, then a default suffix of 00 is used, although the system operator can optionally be allowed to override these selections at load time (if the option in IEASYSxx includes OPI = YES).

Configuration files of particular significance to security within SYS1.PARMLIB, where the characters 'aa' or 'bb' denote the suffix specified (or defaulted) in IEASYS00 are illustrated in Figure 7.4.

Given some understanding of the aspects of MVS that are being defined in these PARMLIB members, many of which are within the TCB of MVS, it should be clear that great care needs to be exercised in configuring and protecting the contents of SYS1.PARMLIB.

IEASYS entry	Parmlib Member	Purpose of PARMLIB member
SCH = aa	SCHEDaa	Includes Program Properties Table
CON = aa	CONSOLaa	Define MVS operating consoles
SSN = aa	IEFSSNaa	Defines non-dynamic subsystems
CMD = aa	COMMNDaa	Automatic commands after IPL
LNK = (aa,bb)	LNKLSTaa LNKLSTbb	Lists of libraries included in the link list
LPA = (aa,bb)	LPALSTaa LPALSTbb	Lists of libraries included in the LPA list
MLPA = (aa,bb)	IEALPAaa IEALPAbb	Lists of modules to appear in the MLPA, specifying their load library
FIX = aa	IEAFIXaa	Lists of modules to appear in the FLPA, specifying their load library
APF = aa	IEAAPFaa	Lists of libraries forming the APF list
SVC = aa	IEASVCaa	Defines additional SVCs
SMF = aa	SMFPRMaa	SMF configuration parameters

Figure 7.4 SYS1.PARMLIB Configuration Files

The dynamic nature of most MVS systems is such that regular changes are made to MVS by systems programming staff. This tends to be reflected in the rate of change to SYS.PARMLIB. Assurances of security in such environments are somewhat transitory, and hence many large installations make a regular practice of conducting security reviews or penetration tests of their MVS systems.

Common Protection Flaws in MVS

In this section we describe a number of protection flaws commonly found in MVS systems. I cannot claim these are representative of MVS systems in general, but certainly can claim that they occur in practice.

Poor access controls on APF libraries

Many MVS systems have in excess of 50 APF libraries, introduced as needed by a particular software product. All too often the access controls on one or more of these allows them to be updated and compromised by non-systems staff (often access control rules are defined to cover a set of files of which the APF library is just one, and this gets overlooked when the library is added to the APF list).

Normally only a minimum number of individuals would need update access to APF libraries, typically only system programmers. Some sites deny anybody update access outside of scheduled maintenance periods, and others log and account for all update activity to APF libraries.

It is hard to conceive of circumstances in which hundreds or thousands of users should be allowed update access to any APF libraries. When such things are encountered they are usually the result of oversight.

Poor access controls on ther MVS system libraries

Various files used by or containing parts of MVS, such as SYS1.NUCLEUS, SYS1.LPALIB or SYS1.UADS sometimes manage to get overlooked when it comes to access controls. Normally all of these should be well protected against updating.

No access controls at all

Some sites choose to run MVS with no form of access control software at all, relying on MVS dataset passwords or luck to prevent security breaches.

Poor configured JES subsystems

The fact that JES and MVS operator commands can be embedded in JCL often gets overlooked so that anybody who can submit batch jobs can issue these commands.

User written APF programs

APF authorised programs that are made widely available (because they are in an APF library that many users can read or because they are in the LPA) may be designed to by-pass normal MVS controls. If they are then there is probably a need to include some additional form of control over these functions within the program. If these controls are deficient or lacking, then they probably introduce security flaws. Locally written APF authorised TSO commands raise similar issues.

Missing APF libraries

If an APF library is declared (in IEAAPFxx) as existing on a certain disk then it ought to be there. If it is not, then anybody who can create a library of the defined name on that volume has their own personal APF library to play with.

User written SVCs

IBM documentation describes design and coding criteria that should be observed in user written SVCs. The need for these should be fairly clear from the examples mentioned earlier in this book about penetration testing.

The classic 'faux pas' with user written SVCs is an SVC that unauthorised callers can invoke, which sets the caller into authorised mode and then returns control to the caller. Anyone who can invoke the SVC gets authorised status and can then do pretty well anything they want. The usual issues concerning validation of user supplied addresses also apply.

Incorrectly installed software products

Some software products, such as database management systems, require to use privileged functions for legitimate purposes. Usually the need to preserve MVS integrity has been understood and considered in the design and implementation of the product.

If, for example, a product requires to be installed with an SVC that only APF authorised callers can invoke, it should be installed in precisely that fashion. It sometimes appears to be the case that this sort of issue slips through because the product functions correctly, if unauthorised callers can invoke the SVC, and so superficially it has been 'properly' installed.

Access control to MVS SMP/E datasets

The various libraries and files that are used for generating and maintaining MVS, including macro libraries, assembler and link editor programs, must be access-protected to prevent them from being altered so that security flaws are not introduced when they are next used. In practice, however, this does not usually constitute a major problem. System programming departments tend to have these fairly well protected, probably because the need to share them with other users doesn't arise, so simple and appropriate access control rules are established and maintained.

Access control software poorly configured

All the access control packages have several notations of privilege that allow certain user-ids to by-pass the normal rule based controls. Often there are vulnerabilities associated with these, for example privileged user-ids that don't require so much as a password check to run a job under them. These are generally due to oversight, but clearly the consequences are potentially dramatic.

7.3 UNIX OPERATING SYSTEMS

The UNIX Operating Systems is a multi-tasking, multi-user operating system that was originally developed at Bell Laboratories in the early 1970s, and rapidly gained favour in academic circles. It was intended to be portable between different hardware architectures with minimal effort, and has indeed been implemented on an enormous number of computers (albeit disguised under a variety of names).

Throughout the 1970s and 1980s, two main types of UNIX have existed. One stream has been based on the UNIX systems developed and distributed by AT&T, the other has been based on the versions developed and supported by the University of California at Berkeley known as the BSD versions. During this time many extensions and enhancements have been made to the basic UNIX facilities, and indeed the existence of the BSD versions is originally due to enhancements sponsored under the American DARPA scheme.

During the late 1980s there was a dramatic increase in interest in UNIX that extended well beyond academia. Interest in computer networking had increased significantly, and UNIX was by then well established in the networking and graphics workstation markets. Interest in Open Systems Interconnection was also increasing, and people were looking for standard environments to support the aims of OSI. UNIX appeared to offer a solution to many of the problems of software portability and interconnection, and was seized upon by computer users and computer vendors alike.

There has been an entertaining power struggle conducted between the two major bodies that develop and supply UNIX, now known as the Open Software Foundation and UNIX International. A certain amount of commercial interest is involved in the competition between these groups, with most of the large computer manufacturers belonging to one or the other (some belong to both for good measure). Both bodies are aiming to provide 'standardised' UNIX, that allows users to overcome the incompatibilities that existed between AT&T and BSD versions, and which conforms to the POSIX standards ratified by the IEEE (which is supposed to describe a generic interface for operating systems, but reads very much like the UNIX system call manual). Both bodies are competing to provide the better implementation, with names like System V Version 4 from UNIX International, and OSF/1 from the Open Software Foundation (based on the Mach operating system developed at Carnegie Mellon University). Although a 'common' base might sound ideal, competition itself tends to result in advances and improvements, and may therefore not be such a bad thing.

In the case of UNIX systems, one of the influencing factors that has led to the difference seen between so many vendors of UNIX products is the TCSEC itself. The standard UNIX operating system does not score highly against the TCSEC, for example, it does not provide sufficient audit trails for level C2, so various suppliers have enhanced their products in these areas. Future versions of UNIX are aiming to redress this position — in particular UNIX System V Release 4 Enhanced Security is aiming for TCSEC level B2 evaluation.

The UNIX Kernel

The UNIX kernel provides a basic TCB, protected by the addressing primitives of the machine being used. Entry into the kernel is made by issuing system calls from non-kernel programs. The kernel implements the more important of the abstractions that are relevant to security in UNIX based systems. These include files, processes, pipes and special files.

Files

UNIX supports several different types of file that are important to its security. In addition to the normal concept of a file as a collection of data held on a disk, UNIX allows devices such as terminals to be treated as files and provides a mechanism known as a pipe, which allows processes to communicate through a file-like interface.

UNIX attempts to disguise the difference between types of file by providing a common presentation of a file as a sequence of one byte characters. This allows a program to read or write from disk files, or terminals without needing to be rewritten, and allows programs to be connected via pipes to perform complex functions. UNIX does not insist on preserving this image of a file, and block oriented file manipulation is also supported where relevant.

Directories

Files are organised by grouping them into directories. A directory is a collection of files, some of which may also be directories. (Actually a directory is essentially a file containing a list of filenames and I-nodes).

All of the directories in a UNIX system form a single hierarchy, the top of which is the root directory of the disk partition from which the UNIX system was loaded. All of the other disks are attached in the root disk hierarchy. The effect of this is to create a single hierarchy of directories, starting from the root node, which can be selected using the name '/'. From this point, any individual file can be selected by specifying a path from the root node, down through the hierarchy of directories until the file itself is found. Filenames that give this complete path through the file system hierarchy are known as 'absolute path names'.

For convenience and flexibility, UNIX also supports the concept of 'current directories' and 'relative path names'. This allows a process to select a directory as its current directory, and then to use filenames relative to the current directory. For example, suppose that directory /usr/gos1/ncc contains the two files /usr/gos1/ncc/unix and /usr/gos1/ncc/mvs. Rather than having to quote the absolute path name each time we want to refer to one of these files, we can establish /usr/gos1/ncc as the current directory, and then refer to the files simply as UNIX and MVS.

Processes

Every process in a UNIX system is associated with a user, and with a user group. The User Identification Number, usually referred to simply as a UID, associates a process with a user. The user is associated with a UID value when logging on to the system. Processes are associated with UIDs so that access controls can be used to control access to objects such as files, directories and devices.

A process is also associated with a user group through the Group Identification Number, or GID.

The UID value of zero is treated as a sort of 'magic number' on most UNIX systems. The code that applies access controls based on UID values will allow whatever access a process running with a UID of zero requests, irrespective of file modes. This 'super user' privilege makes the users that have a UID value of zero a prime target for attempts to penetrate UNIX system security and is widely recognised as a weakness in UNIX systems. Versions of UNIX that aim to improve its overall security often replace this convention with something less risky.

In most systems that recognise the zero UID privilege, the user 'root' exists for use by system administrators and has an associated UID of zero.

Passwords and Logons

When users sign onto UNIX they must identify themselves and provide a password to authenticate their identity. UNIX stores information concerning users and their passwords in a file called /etc/passwd. This file contains one line per user, with each line broken into fields separated by colons. Fields of significance within /etc/passwd are:

- a one way encrypted form of the user's password;

- a timestamp for when the password was last changed;

- the user's logon value;

- the user's UID and GID values;

- the user's logon directory;

- the shell program made available after successful logon.

Some of the information in the /etc/passwd file is used by standard UNIX commands, for such purposes as translating UID values into logon names. For this reason the /etc/passwd file can normally be read by all users (its file mode makes it readable by others).

The fact that encrypted passwords can be read is not a problem provided that the difficulty of systematically determining a password value is great, and the design of UNIX attempted to ensure this. Several techniques were used, such as using a deliberately inefficient encryption routine based on the design of the DES algorithm (actually a different algorithm, so DES hardware implementations do not offer a way to overcome the UNIX routine's inefficiency) and mixing timestamps in with passwords before they are encrypted.

The timestamp, or 'salt' technique is interesting because it increases the difficulty of finding passwords by encrypting a series of words and comparing the results against the contents of /etc/passwd. For example, if there were one hundred logons defined in /etc/passwd, and we knew that one of the passwords was the string 'secret', we could not just encrypt 'secret' and compare the results against each encrypted password. Instead, we would have to obtain the timestamp from each entry, append this to 'secret' and encrypt the result. The result is that to see if a given word has been used as a password somewhere within /etc/passwd we have to encrypt it n times, where n is the number of entries in /etc/passwd.

In spite of these attempts to make password-guessing difficult, the power of modern computers and the fundamental unreliability of user chosen passwords has resulted in a number of successful attacks against /etc/passwd. In order to help redress some of the inherent pasword weaknesses, some versions of UNIX provide a degree of password management. Typical examples include insisting on a mixture of alphabetic and numeric characters and enforced /etc/passwd with a 'shadow' password file (such as /etc/shadow on UNIX V.4). A shadow password file is used to contain the encrypted passwords, and /etc/passwd contains random values. This allows commands to refer to /etc/passwd, while the mode of the shadow password file can prevent it from being widely read.

File Modes

Each file and directory on UNIX has owner and access control data associated with it (stored in an object called an I-node).

The owner of a file is the value of the UID of the process that created the file. In addition to this, each file has an owning group associated with it. The owning group for a file can be derived in two different ways. One approach is to use the effective GID of the process that created the file, the other is to take the value of the owning group of the directory within which the file was created. Different versions of UNIX vary in this report.

Each file and directory is thus associated with a specific UID and GID value. This association is used as the basis for access controls for UNIX files, which can be associated with the file's owner, the file's owning group and 'everybody else', known respectively as 'user', 'group' and 'other' (or 'world') permissions.

For each of these three categories, UNIX allows access to a file to be granted in combinations of three modes:

— r, meaning read access is allowed;

- w, meaning the file can be accessed for writing;

- x, meaning the contents of the file can be executed.

Thus, the access available to processes running with the UID value of the file's owner can be restricted to one or more of *read, write* and *execute* access. Similarly, we can restrict the access available to processes running with the group owner of the file, and control the access available to processes that do not fall into either of these categories. These access permissions are normally expressed in the form of a sequence of nine characters, which make up a crude form of ACL:

rwxrwxrwx

The first three characters apply to the file owner, the second three to the group owner and the final three to 'other'. These characters are either present or absent, with absent characters appearing as '−', indicating that the corresponding access right is not available.

In the example above, all three categories of user can read, write and execute the file. If, for example, users in the 'other' category were able only to execute the file, and nobody was allowed to write to it, the file mode would be represented by:

r−xr−x−−x

Each character position actually represents a bit that can be set within an I-node when the associated permission is available. It is quite common to represent file modes directly using these bit positions expressed as an octal number. Thus, user permissions of 'r−x' correspond to a bit pattern of '101', which can be represented by the octal number 5. The permissions 'r−xr−x−−x' above can also be represented as the octal number 551, and the chmod command will accept either form of expression.

File modes are initially set using a mask set up in the shell. The mask is specified using the umask command. The file mode can subsequently be changed using the chmod command, but only by the owner of the file.

An important consideration for UNIX security is that executable files should be protected such that they cannot be corrupted or overwritten with bad code.

This applies to standard UNIX system utilities that anybody might execute, and to anything that a 'privileged' user might execute.

Imagine that a user 'thief' wants to get access to some file on the system, but the mode of the file in question prevents him doing so. One approach 'thief' might adopt is to alter a program that user 'honest' can execute. When 'honest' calls the corrupt program, the program is able to detect that it has been called by 'honest', and if 'honest' can access the file, the program is able to manipulate the file on 'thief's' behalf. This is not as unlikely as it might sound. Programs such as this are known as 'mines' on UNIX, and may be disguised as standard utilities (in which case they are a type of *Trojan Horse program*, since 'honest' need never be aware of their covert functions). Indeed, some of the earliest experiments with computer viruses were conducted on UNIX systems in this manner, relying simply on the fact that system administrators would experiment with new programs found on the system, and whenever they did the program was invoked with root privilege. It is interesting to note that the use of mandatory integrity controls would prevent this type of problem — if the system refused to execute the low integrity program on behalf of a high integrity caller.

Another area in which file modes play a crucial role in UNIX security is in protecting the 'device' files that allow direct access to device drivers. Device files are normally stored exclusively in the /dev directory (or one of its subdirectories). The ability to read or write to a disk device file, for example, allows a user to read or write to the disk ignoring its organisation into I-nodes, directories and files. This results in file modes applied to those directories and files being ignored.

File modes apply to directories as well as files (in fact, a directory is a file that contains a list of file and directory names that are 'within' the directory). In the case of directories, the access modes are interpreted differently:

- r means the contents of the directory can be listed;

- x means the directory can be searched in evaluating path names;

- w means files can be placed within or removed from the directory.

Directory modes often get overlooked by system administrators, which can lead to some nasty security problems. In particular, allowing *write* mode to a directory means that programs within it can be replaced by other versions. This could result in unsuspecting users invoking the replaced program and exposing themselves to whatever the effects of the program happen to be.

Real and Effective UID and GID values

In many versions of UNIX a process has not one, but three UID and GID values. The reason for providing three versions of each is to support the mechanisms that allow UID and GID values to be changed when a new process is created, or when a process requests that it be changed. When one process creates another, it will usually be for the purpose of executing a specific program in the 'child' process. The name of the program is passed to the UNIX kernel, which arranges for the program to be copied into the child process. In the normal course of events the child process will execute using the same UID and GID values as the process that created it, but sometimes it is necessary to use different values.

A good example is the *ps* program. This program needs to read a device file that gives it access to the computer's memory, from which it obtains details about the processes current in the system. Access to this device file is not normally allowed to users in general, but the limited use of the data available from memory that is made by the *ps* program is not normally considered harmful. In other words, the *ps* program can be allowed access to the device file, but the caller of *ps* is not allowed access to the device file. UNIX allows a program to run with a different UID, and/or GID, from that of the process that called it. This allows the *ps* program to run in a process that has access to the device file it needs, while the UID and GID of its caller do not allow this access. The mechanism that supports this is the SUID and SGID mechanism.

The SUID mechanism is selected when an executable file is loaded into a new process, if the SUID bit is set on in the executable file's mode bits. If the bit is on, the process' UID will be that of the executable file's owner, rather than that of the calling process.

Another way that a process' UID and GID values can be changed, is that the 'setuid' and 'setgid' system calls provided by the kernel can be used to change them. For most processes, these system calls will only allow the UID and GID to be changed to the values of the UID and GID of the parent process. In most cases this will be equal to the current values of the UID and GID, which were inherited from the parent. If the child process is executing a program that had the set UID bit set, however, the values will be different. In this case the child process can reset its UID that that of its parent process, and on some UNIX systems can toggle backwards and forwards between the two values.

As usual, root processes, that is those with a UID of zero, can use the setuid system call to change their current UID value to anything they like. These mechanisms depend on the existence of three UID and GID values in each process. The first of these values is the 'real' UID or GID, and is always set to that of the parent process. There are also two 'effective' UID and GID values.

The second of these two effective UID (or GID) values is the one that the UNIX kernel uses when checking file modes, and both the first and second UID (GID) values are reset when a SUID file is executed. For most processes, all three versions will be the same, but for a SUID process, the real UID will be equal to its parent process UID, and both of its effective UID values will be equal to the executable program file's owner. The SUID process may then call the SUID system call, which will allow the second effective UID value to be changed to the value of the real UID (and on some systems, allow it to be changed back again to the value of the first effective UID).

UNIX Shells

The UNIX shell programs provide a command interpreter for users wishing to run UNIX programs and utilities from terminals attached to the system.

There are several versions of the shell in common use, these being the Bourne, C and Korn shells. They have much in common in the sense that the utilities they make available, together with their basic syntax and features, all have a distinctly UNIX flavour. They all provide features for redirecting input and output from programs into or out of files or other processes, and they all allow sequences of commands to be stored and executed from files as a 'shell script' procedure. They all recognise and maintain standard 'shell variables' expected within UNIX, such as PATH for specifying where the kernel should search for programs to be run and IFS for specifying delimiters for elements of command line arguments.

There are differences between them, for example, the C shell allows elements of previous command line to be recalled within the current command line. For our purposes here, we need not be concerned with these details, but

will concentrate upon the fundamental aspects of the shell programs, which
are largely similar. The purpose of the shell program is to read lines of input,
to provide some simple programming constructs (such as string variables,
arguments to shell scripts and logical operators) and to invoke UNIX programs.
Much of the function of the shell programs is concerned with handling files,
and features are provided for pattern matching between filenames and for
redirecting program input and output to files (recall that UNIX presents devices
such as terminals, as files, so a program need not be aware it is reading from
a file instead of a terminal).

The shell is itself just a program running in a process, with its standard input
being obtained from a terminal. This process was created by the 'init' process,
which is a standard process responsible for many routine operations concerned
with starting, stopping and managing a running UNIX system. When the shell
starts a command on behalf of a user, it requests the UNIX kernel to create a
new process to run the program in (at least in the normal course of events).
Several aspects of the shell programs of these are introduced in the following
sections.

The PATH variable

The PATH variable is one of several string variables maintained in the
environment provided to shell programs. This has the effect that when one
process running a shell program forks, another, the child process inherits the
PATH variable from its parent (UNIX uses the term 'forking' to describe what
is more normally referred to as process spawning). The PATH variable specifies
a list of directories to be searched when attempting to locate a program for
running, when the absolute pathname for the command is not supplied.
Entries in this list are separated by colons.

The PATH shell variable is easily altered, so it is unwise for any privileged
programs to rely upon it being correctly set. It is possible to cause privileged
code to pick up bogus versions of programs by changing the PATH variable to
include a directory containing the bogus program.

A null entry in the PATH variable refers to the process' current directory.
Including the current directory in the PATH variable is dangerous if the current
directory is ever set to a directory whose contents are of doubtful integrity,
because any bogus versions of programs appearing in the directory may be
invoked by unwary shell users or programs that they run.

Programs that run SUID to a privileged logon such as root are often the target of attempts to cause bogus programs to be picked up and invoked. A program picked up in this manner will run with an effective UID of its caller and be able to usurp the callers privilege. For this reason it is good practice to use full pathnames when calling programs from such logons, and to avoid placing the current directory in the PATH variable.

Restricted shells

Restricted shells are intended to securely confine a process within its home directory, preventing the current directory from being changed. The restricted shell user is prevented from assigning to the PATH variable, which is assigned when the user's profile file is automatically executed during logon processing. In practice, a more reliable approach is centered on the chroot command, and this approach has been adopted by at least one UNIX system aiming for TCSEC evaluation.

The chroot approach re-defines a process' view of the file system root, so that when it refers to '/', which is normally the root of the file system, it actually gets a directory somewhere lower down in the file system. This is the highest point in the file system that the process can refer to, since there is nothing above 'root'.

A consequence of this, is that any commands the process is allowed to execute must appear below its perceived root directory. Many commands and programs will expect to find standard directories and files in the usual place, relative to the root directory, so it is often necessary to mirror the expected file system structure under the perceived root directory.

Networking

UNIX has always provided mechanisms allowing a collection of systems to be linked together over a network. Originally the facilities provided were limited to simple file transfer and remote logon techniques, upon which the UNIX electronic mail features were built (often called the Basic Networking Facilities). Later enhancements to the basic networking mechanisms included networked file systems. There are two main varieties of these in common use, known as NFS and RFS. They allow a UNIX file server system to export parts of its file system for use by client systems. (Strictly the server need not be a UNIX system, but it would need to implement the protocols required by the network file service and to present an image of a UNIX file system to the clients).

Today, there is a wide variety of networking features available on UNIX systems, which are often used to support networks of powerful workstations. RPC mechanisms of various sorts, general purpose network interfaces (ports, streams etc), OSI interfaces and security enhancements for these (such as 'secure NFS, Strongbox for Mach and Kerberos from MIT) abound. One may ask then, if solid security features are available for networked UNIX systems, why networked based attacks on UNIX systems have been so successful. The infamous 'Internet Worm' program, for example, was able to spread across most of the Internet network largely by attacking flawed network code and password-guessing.

The weakness exploited by the Internet Worm were several, notably:

- poor system administration, failing to address known and publicised security flaws;

- bad choices of password values by users;

- lax practice by users, allowing unconstrained access to their logon from selected remote systems on the network;

- security flaws in network code (primarily failure to perform bound checking, through choice of an inappropriate C library routine).

One of the reasons that the Internet Worm attack succeeded was because it was relatively sophisticated. Also, it attacked the inherent vulnerability of password mechanisms and exploited common administrative weaknesses in UNIX networking. UNIX is not alone in its vulnerability in these areas. We must hope that the influence of security evaluation criteria will assist in removing the type of coding flaws exploited by the Internet Worm from this and from any other future operating systems in which we place trust.

Notes:

1   IBM 81a, IBM 83a
2   Dei 84a
3   IBM 81a

(*see* Reference section).

References

ANS 87   *ANSA Reference Manual*, Cambridge, CB2 1JP, UK.

Ame 87   Ames R S, Gasser M and Schell R R, *Security Kernel Design and Implementation: An Introduction in 'Computer Network Security'*, IEEE Computer Society Press, 1987, pp 142–150.

Att 76   Attanasio, C R, Markstein P W and Phillips R J, *Penetrating an Operating System: A Study of VM/370 Integrity, IBM System Journal*, 1976, Vol 11, No 1.

Bad 89   Badger L, *A Model for Specifying Multi-granularity Integrity Policies*, Proceedings of the 1989 Symposium on Security and Privacy, IEEE Press, 1989, pp 269–277.

Bar 84   Barton F B and Barton M S, *User Friendly Password Methods for Computer-mediated Information Systems, Computers and Security 3*, North-Holland, 1984, pp 186–195.

Bel 77   Bell D E and LaPadula L J, *Secure Computer Systems: Mathematical Foundations and Model*, The MITRE Corporation, 1977.

Ben 85   Benzel T C V and Tavilla D A, *Trusted Software Verification: A Case Study Symposium on Security and Privacy*, IEEE 1985, pp 14–31.

Ber 79   Berson T and Barksdale G, *KSOS-Development Methodology for a Secure Operating System*, Proceedings of the National Computer Conference, AFIPS Press 1979, Vol 48.

Ber 84   Berman A, *Effective Password Protection*, Canadian Datasystems, November 1984.

Bir 84   Birrell A D and Nelson B J, *Implementing Remote Procedure Calls*, ACM Transactions on Computer Systems, February 1984, Vol 2, No 1.

Bir 85   Birrell A, *Secure Communications Using Remote Procedure Calls*, ACM Transactions on Computer Systems, February 1985, 3(1), pp 1–14.

Boe 85   Boebert W E, Kain R Y, Young W D and Hansohn S A, *Secure ADA Target: Issues, System Design and Verification*, Proceedings of the 1985 Symposium on Security and Privacy, IEEE Computer Society Press, April 1985.

Boe 87   Boebert W E, Kain R Y and Young W D, *Secure Computing: The Secure ADA Target Approach in 'Computer Network Security'*, IEEE Computer Society Press, 1987, pp 238–254.

Che 81   Cheheyl M H, Gasser M, Huff G A and Millen J K, *Verifying Security, Computing Surveys*, September 1981, Vol 13, No 3.

Coo 84   Cooper J A, *Computer-Security Technology*, Lexington Books, 1984.

Dei 84   Deitel H M, *An Introduction to Operating Systems*, Addison Wesley, 1984.

Den 76   Denning D E, *A Lattice Model of Secure Information Flow, Communications of the ACM*, May 1976, Vol 19, No 5.

Den 82   Denning D E, *Cryptography and Data Security*, Addison-Wesley, 1982.

DoD 83   Department of Defense Computer Security Center, *Department of Defence Trusted Computer System Evaluation Criteria*, Fort George G. Meade, CSC-STD-001-83.

DoD 87   The National Computer Security Center, *Trusted Network Interpretation of the TCSEC*, Fort George G. Meade, DoD 5200.28-STD.

Dou 83   Douglas L J, (ed) *Audit and Control of Systems Software*, NCC Publications, 1983.

DTI 89   DTI Commercial Computer Security Centre, *Overview of Documentation*, Department of Trade and Industry, February 1989, V01-Version 3.0 (draft).

DTI 89   DTI Commercial Computer Security Centre, *Glossary*, *Department of Trade and Industry*, February 1989, V02-Version 3.0 (draft).

DTI 89   DTI Commercial Computer Security Centre, *Security Functionality Manual*, Department of Trade and Industry, February 1989, V21-Version 3.9 (draft).

DTI 89   DTI Commercial Computer Security Centre, *Evaluation Levels Manual*, Department of Trade and Industry, February 1989, V22-Version 3.0 (draft).

DTI 89   DTI Commercial Computer Security Centre, *Evaluation and Certification Manual*, Department of Trade and Industry, February 1989, V23-Version 3.0 (draft).

DTI 89   DTI Commercial Computer Security Centre, *Vendors Code of Practice*, Department of Trade and Industry, October 1989, V31-Version 3.0 (draft).

DTI 89   DTI Commercial Computer Security Centre, *User's Code of Practice*, Department of Trade and Industry, November 1989, V11-Version 3.0 (draft).

ElK 84   El-Kateeb A M, Al-Khayatt S S and Hermiz G S, *A Computer Log-on Technique Using a One-way Function*, Information Age, 1984, Vol 6, No 3.

Eva 74   Evans A and Krantowitz W, *A User Authentication Scheme not Requiring Secrecy in the Computer*, Communications of the ACM, August 1974, Vol 17, No 8.

Fab 74   Fabry R S *Capability Based Addressing*, Communications of the ACM, July 1974, Vol 17, No 7.

Fei 79   Feiertag R J and Neumann P G, *The Foundations of a Provably Secure Operating System (PSOS)*, Proceedings of the National Computer Conference, AFIPS Press, 1979, Vol 48.

FIP 46   Federal Information Processing Standards, *Data Encryption Standard*, US Department of Commerce/National Bureau of Standards, January 1977, Publication 46.

FIP 48   Federal Information Processing Standards, *Guidelines on the Evaluation of Techniques for Automated Personal Identification*, National Bureau of Standards, Publication 48.

FIP 81   Federal Information Processing Standards, *DES Modes of Operation*, US Department of Commerce/National Bureau of Standards, December 1980, Publication 81.

FRA 83   Fraim L J, *SCOMP: A Solution to the MLS Problem*, Proceedings of IFIP Security Conference, 1983, pp 275–286.

Gai 78   Gai J, *Easy Entry: The Password Encryption Problem, ACM Operating Systems Review*, July 1978, Vol 12, No 3, pp 54-59.

Gif 82   Gifford D K, *Cryptographic Sealing for Information Secrecy and Authenticaiton*, Communications of the ACM, April 1982, Vol 25, No 4, pp 274–286.

Gol 79   Gold B, Linde R, Peeler, R, Schaefer M, Sceid J and Ward P, A Security Retrofit to VM/370, Proceedings of the National Computer Conference, AFIPS Press, 1979, Vol 48.

Gol 84   Gold B D, Linde R R and Cudney P F, *KVM/370 in Retrospect, Symposium on Security and Privacy*, IEEE, 1984, pp 13–23.

Gra 68   Graham R M, *Protection in an Information Processing Utility*, Communications of the ACM, May 1968, Vol 11, No 5.

Gra 72   Graham G S and Denning P J, Protection-Principles and Practice, Spring Joint Computer Conference, 1972.

Har 76   Harrison, M A, and Ruzzo, W L, *Protection in Operating Systems*, Communications of the ACM, August 1976, Vol 9, No 8, pp 461–471.

Has 84   Haskett J A, *Pass-Algorithms: A User Validation Scheme Based on Knowledge of Secret Algorithms*, Communications of the ACM, August 1984, Vol 27, No 8.

Heb 80   Hebbard B et al, *A Penetration Analysis of the Michigan Terminal System*, ACM Operating System Review, June 1980, Vol 14, No 1.

IBM 81   International Business Machines, *Statement of MVS System Integrity*, IBM, October 1981, ULET ZP81-0801.

IBM 83   International Business Machines, *Statement of System Integrity, VM/System Product Release 3 and Companion VM/SP High Performance Option Release*, ULET 5664−147, 5664−174, *IBM Programming Information Customer Letter*, June 1983.

IBM 88   International Business Machines, *Multi-level Security Statement of Direction*, IBM, March 1988, ULET ZA88-0147.

ISO 89   Information Processing Systems — *Open Systems Interconnection — Basic Reference Model — Part 2: Security Architecture*, ISO 7498−2.

ITSEC 91 Information Technology Evaluation Criteria, Version 1.2, 28 June 1991.

Jon 76   Jones A K, Lipton R J and Snyder L, *A Linear Time Algorithm for Deciding Security*, Proceedings of the 17th Annual Symposium on Foundations of Computer Science, 1976.

Jon 79   Jones A K, *The Object Model: A Conceptual Tool for Structuring Software, Operating Systems: An Advanced Course*, Bayer R, Graham R M and Seegmuller G, Spriner-Verlag, 1979, pp 7−10.

Jon 79   Jones A K, *Protection Mechanisms and the Enforcement of Security Policies, Operating Systems: An Advanced Course*, Bayer R, Graham R M and Seegmuller G, Spriner-Verlag, 1979, pp 228−251.

Jue 83   Jueneman R R, Matyas S M and Meyer C H, *Message Authentication With Manipulation Detection Codes*, Proceedings of the IEEE Symposium on Security and Privacy, April 1983.

Kar 88   Karger P A, *Implementing Commercial Data Integrity With Secure Capabilities*, Proceedings of the 1988 Symposium on Security and Privacy, IEEE Press, 1988, pp 130−139.

Kem 82　Kemmerer R A, *A Practical Approach to Identifying Storage and Timing Channels*, Proceedings of the IEEE 1982 Symposium on Security and Privacy, pp 66–73.

Kin 87　King D, *Cryptographic File Storage*, ICL Technical Journal, November 1987, Vol 5, Issue 4, pp 699–709.

Koe 84　Koehring J, *Automatic Identity Verificiation*, Information Age, April 1984, Vol 6, No 2.

Lam 69　Lampson B W, *Dynamic Protection Structures*, Fall Joint Computer Conference, 1969.

Lam 73　Lampson B W, *A Note on the Confinement Problem*, Communications of the ACM, October 1973, Vol 16, No 10.

Lam 74　Lampson B W, *Protection, ACM Operating Systems Review*, January 1974, Vol 8, No 1, pp 18–24.

Lan 81　Landwehr C E, *Formal Models for Computer Security*, Computing Surveys, September 1981, Vol 13, No 3.

Lee 88　Lee T M P, *Using Mandatory Integrity to Enforce 'Commercial' Security*, Proceedings of the 1988 Symposium on Security and Privacy, IEEE Press, 1988, pp 140–146.

Lin 75　Linde R R, *Operating Systems Penetration*, National Computer Conference, 1975, pp 361–366.

Lip 82　Lipner S B, *Non-discretionary Controls for Commercial Applications*, Proceedings of the 1982 Symposium on Security and Privacy, IEEE Press, 1982, pp 2–19.

MCC 79　McCauley E J, *KOS: The Design of a Secure Operating System*, Conference Proceedings, Vol 48, 1979, pp 345–353.

Mey 82　Meyer C H and Matyas S M, Cryptography: A New Dimension in Computer Data Security, Wiley-Interscience, 1982.

Mor 79　Morris R and Thomson K, *Password Security: A Case History*, Communications of the ACM, November 1979, Vol 22, No 11.

Nee 72   Needham R M, *Protection Systems and Protection Implementations*, Fall Joint Computer Conference, 1972.

Nee 78   Needham R M and Schroeder M D, *Using Encryption for Authentication in Large Networks of Computers*, Communications of the ACM, December 1978, Vol 21, No 12.

Nee 87   Needham R M and Schroeder M D, *Authentication Revisited*, ACM Operating Systems Review, January 1987, Vol 21, No 1.

Osh 88   O'Shea G F G, *Controlling the Dependence of User Access Control Mechanisms on Correctness of User Identification*, The Computer Journal, December 1988, Vol 31, No 6, pp 503–509.

Otw 87   Otway D, and Rees O, *Efficient and Timely Mutual Authentication*, ACM Operating Systems Review, January 1987, Vol 21, No 1.

Pet 83   Peterson J L, and Silberschatz A, *Operating System Concepts*, *Addison-Wesley, 1983.*

Pop 74   Popek G J, *Protection Structures*, Computer, June 1974, pp 22–23.

Pop 79   Popek G J, Kampe M, Kline C S, Stoughton A, Urban M and Waton E, *UCLA Secure UNIX*, Proceedings of the National Computer Conference, AFIPS Press, 1979, Vol 48.

Pop 79   Popek G J and Kline C S, *Issues in Kernel Design, Operating Systems: An Advanced Course*, Bayer R, Graham R M and Seegmuller G, Spriner-Verlag, 1979, pp 209–227.

Por 82   Porter, S N, *A Password Extension for Improved Human Factors*, Computers and Security, 1982, pp 54–56.

Riv 78   Rivest R L, Shamir A and Adleman L, *A Method for Obtaining Digital Signatures and Public Key Cryptosystems*, Communications of the ACM, December 1981, Vol 15, No 5, pp 12–21.

Rus 81   Rushby J M, *Design and Verification of Secure Systems, ACM Operating Systems Review*, December 1981, Vol 15, No 5, pp 12–21.

Rus 83   Rushby J and Randell B, *A Distributed Secure System*, IEEE Computer, July 1983, Vol 16, No 7.

Sal 74   Saltzer J H, *Protection and the Control of Information Sharing in Multics*, Communications of the ACM, Vol 17, No 7, 1974.

Sal 75   Saltzer J H and Schroeder M D, *The Protection of Information in Computer Systems*, Proceedings of the IEEE, September 1975, Vol 63, No 9.

Sch 77   Schroeder M D, Clark D D and Saltzer J H, *The Multics Kernel Design Project ACM, Operating Systems Review*, November 1977, Vol 11, No 5.

Sch 83   Schweitzer J A, *Computer Security: Make Your Passwords More Effective*, Edpacs, February 1983.

Sha 48   Shannon C E, *Mathematical Theory of Communication*, Bell System Technical Journal, July 1984.

Sha 51   Shannon C E, *Prediction and Entropy of Printed English*, Bell System Technical Journal, January 1951.

Sil 83   Silverman J M, *Reflecting on the Verification of the Security of an Operating System Kernel*, Proceedings of the 9th ACM Symposium on Operating System Principles, October 1983.

Tan 85   Tanenbaum A S and Van Renesse R, *Distributed Operating Systems*, ACM Computing Surveys, December 1983, Vol 17, No 4.

Tan 87   Tanenbaum A S, *Operating Systems: Design and Implementation*, Prentice Hall International, 1987.

Wik 81   Wilkinson A L et al, *A Penetration Analysis of a Burroughs Large System*, ACM Operating Systems Review, January 1981, Vol 15, No 1.

Woo 77   Wood H M, *The Use of Passwords and Controlling Access to Remote Computer Systems and Services*, National Computer Confernece, 1977.

Woo 83   Wood C C, *Effective Information System Security with Password Controls*, Computers and Security, Elsevier Science, 1983, Vol 2.

Woo 85   Wood M B, *Computer Access Control*, NCC Publications, 1985.

Bibliography

The following are suggested for further reading:

Bayer R, Graham R M and Seegmuller G, *Operating Systems: An Advanced Course*, Spriner-Verlag, 1979.

Deital H M, *An Introduction to Operating Systems*, Addison-Wesley, 1984.

Denning D E, *Cryptography and Data Security*, Addison-Wesley, 1982.

Douglas L J (editor) *Audit and Control of Systems Software*, NCC Publications, 1983.

Lister A M, *Fundamentals of Operating Systems*, Macmillan, 1975.

Meyer C H and Matyas S M, *Cryptography: A New Dimension in Computer Data Security*, Wiley-Interscience, 1982.

Peterson J L and Silberschatz A, *Operating System Concepts*, Addison-Wesley, 1983.

Sennet C, *High Integrity Software*, Pitman, 1989.

Tanenbaum A S, *Operating Systems: Design and Implementation*, Prentic Hall International Inc, 1987.

Wood M B, *Computer Access Control*, NCC Publications, 1985.

Index